TEAM HANDBALL

Steps to Success

Reita E. Clanton
Assistant Women's 1996 Olympic Team Handball Coach
Head Coach, Team 2000 Women's Team Handball
United States Team Handball Federation
Atlanta, GA

Mary Phyl Dwight
Women's Development Coach
United States Team Handball Federation
Atlanta, GA

Human Kinetics

Library of Congress Cataloging-in-Publication Data

Clanton, Reita E., 1952-
   Team handball : steps to success / Reita E. Clanton, Mary Phyl Dwight.
      p.   cm. -- (Steps to success activity series)
   Includes bibliographical references.
   ISBN 0-87322-411-6
    1. Team handball. I. Dwight, Mary Phyl, 1951-   . II. Title. III. Series.
  GV1017.T4C53   1997
  796.31'2--dc20   96-15149
                                       CIP

ISBN: 0-87322-411-6

Developmental Editor: Judy Patterson Wright, PhD; **Assistant Editors:** John Wentworth and Andrew Smith; **Editorial Assistants:** Jennifer Hemphill and Alecia Mapes Walk; **Copyeditor:** Denelle Eknes; **Proofreader:** Sue Fetters; **Graphic Designer:** Keith Blomberg; **Graphic Artists:** Robert Reuther and Denise Lowry; **Cover Designer:** Jack Davis; **Photographer (cover):** Will Zehr; **Illustrators:** Keith Blomberg and Jennifer Delmotte; **Printer:** Versa Press

Instructional Designer for the Steps to Success Activity Series: Joan N. Vickers, EdD, University of Calgary, Calgary, Alberta, Canada

Human Kinetics books are available at special discounts for bulk purchase. Special editions or book excerpts can also be created to specification. For details, contact the Special Sales Manager at Human Kinetics.

Printed in the United States of America   10 9 8 7 6 5 4 3

Human Kinetics
Web site: www.HumanKinetics.com

United States: Human Kinetics, P.O. Box 5076, Champaign, IL 61825-5076
800-747-4457
e-mail: humank@hkusa.com

Canada: Human Kinetics, 475 Devonshire Road, Unit 100, Windsor, ON N8Y 2L5
800-465-7301 (in Canada only)
e-mail: orders@hkcanada.com

Europe: Human Kinetics, 107 Bradford Road, Stanningley
Leeds LS28 6AT, United Kingdom
+44 (0) 113 255 5665
e-mail: hk@hkeurope.com

Australia: Human Kinetics, 57A Price Avenue, Lower Mitcham, South Australia 5062
08 8277 1555
e-mail: liaw@hkaustralia.com

New Zealand: Human Kinetics, Division of Sports Distributors NZ Ltd.
P.O. Box 300 226 Albany, North Shore City, Auckland
0064 9 448 1207
e-mail: blairc@hknewz.com

Contents

PREFACE

Welcome to the exciting Olympic sport of team handball. Even though millions of people enjoy the sport throughout the world, team handball is an underdeveloped sport in the United States. *Team Handball: Steps to Success* has been written to give you, as a beginning player, the chance to put your enthusiasm for this new sport into action. You start by learning the basic rules and gaining an understanding of the physical requirements in the sport. You need not have a specific body type to be successful in team handball, but excellent all-around physical conditioning and an aggressive competitive desire are necessary. This contact sport blends strength, speed, agility, and endurance in a physically challenging way.

Next, you participate in a progressive program of individual and team skill development. Once you acquire the skills, you practice them in gamelike situations to help learn proper execution under pressure and how to make good decisions. Factors that create gamelike conditions include adding defense, restricting space, limiting time, and inducing physical fatigue. Practice under these conditions helps you develop the intangible qualities of determination and confidence that any good player must possess.

Determining what individual and team skills were essential to expose you to was the hardest part of writing this book. There are many skills we were not able to cover. As a beginning player, covering everything would be overwhelming for you. Unlike Europeans who have played since they were young children, you are likely to be learning team handball for the first time as an older player, as we did. This book is unique from other team handball publications because we remember what it was like to be an experienced athlete in another sport, yet learning team handball for the first time in our twenties. Regardless of your age, this book will provide you with what you need to enjoy the game. Twenty years of playing, coaching, and teaching team handball have taught us what is important for the beginning player. We have taught the game to teachers, coaches, and varsity collegiate athletes and have coached all skill levels of Special Olympics athletes. We included those basic skills, tactics, and strategies that would allow you to play the game quickly and provide the foundation for your development as a player. The basic skills you need to play team handball are the same skills you use for other sports, primarily basketball and baseball or softball, which are probably familiar to you. You will combine your natural athletic skills of running, jumping, throwing, and catching as you develop as a team handball player.

Understanding game tactics and strategies is also important. You will test your decision-making abilities as you experience the rapidly changing action of the game. You will learn how your individual development contributes to the team as a whole. Six court players and a goalie work together, with each player having individual responsibilities that will contribute to the team's success.

Whether you participate for fun and fitness or seriously compete with the dream of someday making an Olympic team, your love for team handball will grow as you experience the game and improve your performance. Use this book to progress through the steps to success at your own pace. Organize a team handball club or league in your area through your school or Park and Recreation Department. Pass on your enthusiasm for team handball by displaying your new skills in games and tournaments. We think you will find that once you start playing the game regularly you will create an individual style of play and develop more advanced techniques.

We believe this project will represent an important point for team handball development in the United States. The 1996 Olympics in Atlanta will create excitement about the sport of team handball. The marketplace needs a quality team handball book for the beginning player, written in English by American teachers and Olympic athletes. *Team Handball: Steps to Success* provides a book that players, teachers, students, and spectators excited about team handball will be able to pick up in a local bookstore or check out of the library.

There are several people we want to thank who have influenced the development and completion of this book. Peter Buehning, former president of the United States Team Handball Federation (USTHF), gave us the opportunity to get involved in this great sport. We were selected to the first USTHF Women's National Team in 1974 and traveled throughout the world competing in the sport. The USTHF also chose us as members of the first Women's U.S. Olympic Team for the 1984 Olympics in Los Angeles. Our sincere appreciation goes to three U.S. National Team coaches who greatly influenced our understanding of the sport and development as players and coaches, Stan Mandroski, Javier Garcia Cuesta, and Claes Hellgren.

Several friends contributed support to this project in a variety of ways. Thanks to Susan Todaro, Sandra Leigh, and Jona Braden for editing and critiquing along the way. Joe Thomas and Mary Carter provided photography for the illustrator of the book. Our thanks go to our families for their encouragement and support of this project, especially our parents Jack and Rudene Clanton and Nelson and Bessie Dwight.

We would like to thank Human Kinetics for taking an interest in team handball and publishing this book. A special thanks to Judy Patterson Wright for all her help and patience while completing the project. It was a lot harder than we had imagined.

THE STEPS TO SUCCESS STAIRCASE

Get ready to climb a staircase—one that will lead you to become an accomplished team handball player. You cannot leap to the top—you get there by climbing one step at a time.

Each of the 12 steps you take is an easy transition from the one before. The first few steps of the staircase provide a solid foundation of basic skills and concepts. As you progress further, you will learn how to combine those seemingly isolated skills. You will learn how to attack the goal, how to decide when to pass and when to shoot, and how you can support your teammates when attacking and defending. As you near the top of the staircase, you'll learn how seven players with individual responsibilities organize as one unit in attack and on defense and how communication contributes to the effectiveness of the team.

Familiarize yourself with this section as well as with The Game of Team Handball, The Playing Court and Equipment, and Appendix A: Simplified Rules. These sections give you a game overview, the physical requirements, the playing area requirements, the size and type of team handballs, and an explanation of the basic rules. The knowledge you gain will help you understand how to set up your practice sessions around the steps. Appendix B provides suggestions for modifying your floor space to create a team handball court.

Follow the same sequence each step (chapter) of the way:

1. Read the explanations of what is covered in the step, why the step is important, and how to execute or perform the step's focus, which may be on basic skills, concepts, tactics, or a combination of the three.

2. Follow the numbered illustrations showing exactly how to position your body to execute each basic skill successfully. There are three general parts to each skill: preparation (getting into a starting position), execution (performing the skill that is the focus of the step), and recovery (reaching a finish position or following through to starting position). These are your keys to success.

3. Look over the common errors that may occur and the recommendations for how to correct them.

4. Practice the drills to help you improve your skills through repetition. Read the directions and the Success Goal for each drill. Then review the Success Checks and practice accordingly. Record your score and compare your performance with the Success Goal for the drill. Because the drills are arranged in an easy-to-difficult progression, you need to meet the Success Goal of each drill before moving on to practice the next one. This sequence is designed specifically to help you achieve continual success. Pace yourself by adjusting the drills to either increase or decrease difficulty, depending on where you are. See the symbol key to the diagrams at the end of this section.

5. As soon as you can reach all the Success Goals for one step, you are ready for a qualified observer—such as your coach or trained partner—to evaluate your basic

skill technique against the step's keys to success. This is a qualitative or subjective evaluation of your basic technique or form, because using correct form can enhance your performance.

6. Repeat these procedures for each of the 12 steps to success. Then rate yourself according to the directions in the Rating Your Total Progress section at the end of the book.

Good luck on your step-by-step journey to developing your team handball skills, building confidence, experiencing success, and having fun!

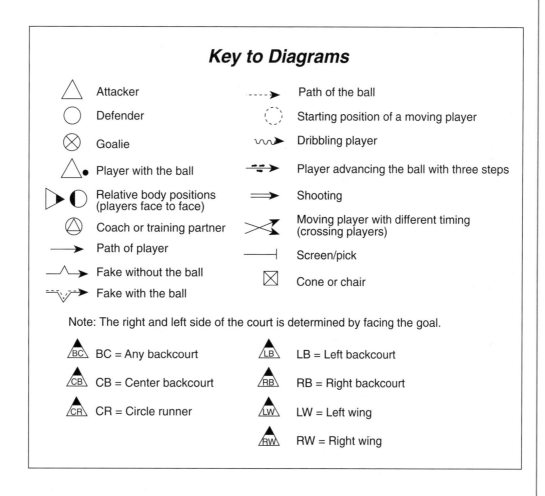

Key to Diagrams

△	Attacker	----▸	Path of the ball
○	Defender	(⌁)	Starting position of a moving player
⊗	Goalie	⌁⌁⌁▸	Dribbling player
△•	Player with the ball	-=-▸	Player advancing the ball with three steps
▷◖	Relative body positions (players face to face)	⟹	Shooting
⊖	Coach or training partner	⤢	Moving player with different timing (crossing players)
⟶	Path of player	⊢	Screen/pick
⟋\⟶	Fake without the ball	⊠	Cone or chair
⟍∨⟶	Fake with the ball		

Note: The right and left side of the court is determined by facing the goal.

▲BC	BC = Any backcourt	▲LB	LB = Left backcourt
▲CB	CB = Center backcourt	▲RB	RB = Right backcourt
▲CR	CR = Circle runner	▲LW	LW = Left wing
		▲RW	RW = Right wing

THE GAME OF TEAM HANDBALL: IT'S NOT OFF THE WALL!

Although popular throughout much of the world, team handball is just emerging in the United States and often suffers from an identity crisis. Most of the world calls the game "handball," but in the United States there is already another sport with that name. Most Americans who hear of team handball envision participants on something like a racquetball court smacking a little black ball with their hands. This vision is not accurate—without a doubt, team handball is *not* off the wall!

Team handball is a dynamic sport that is fun to play and exciting to watch. The sport uses natural athletic skills such as running, jumping, throwing, and catching to provide the action for the game. Players and spectators alike enjoy the fast, continuous play, the body contact, and the goalie action. First-time spectators describe team handball as soccer with your hands, but they also notice elements that remind them of basketball, water polo, and ice hockey.

Playing the Game

Team handball is played between two teams, each with six court players and a goalie, on a court larger than a basketball court. The object of the game is to throw a cantaloupe-sized ball into your opponent's 2-meter by 3-meter goal while defending your goal from attack (see Figure 1). A regulation game is played in 30-minute halves with one 60-second team time-out per half. A coin toss determines which team starts the game with a throw-off. From that point, the action is continuous. The clock stops only for injury, team time-outs, and at the referee's discretion. A successful scoring attempt results in the award of 1 point. Goals scored per game typically range from the upper teens to mid-twenties.

Basic defense protects the goal area by placing all six players around it, forming a wall. A semicircular line 6 meters from the goal marks the goal area. Only the goalie occupies this area, and attackers and defenders must remain outside. Defense technique is similar to basketball with the exception that it allows more contact. Rules permit body contact with the torso, but players may not push, hold, or endanger an opponent in any way. Excessive roughness results in a warning or a 2-minute suspension.

When in attack, players are called backcourts, wings, and circle runners. Passing is the primary way to move the ball in attack. A player may take three steps with the ball before and after dribbling, but while stationary may hold the ball only 3 seconds. The attacking players' task is to find a way over, around, or through the defensive "wall." Players do this using strategies similar to basketball, incorporating the concepts of the screen, pick and

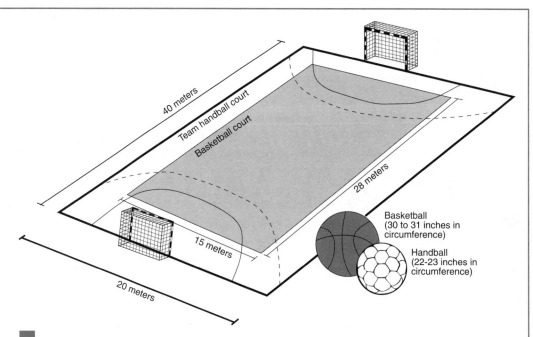

Figure 1 Dimensions in team handball compared to those in basketball. As you see, the team handball court is significantly bigger while the ball is significantly smaller.

roll, and the overload. The offense may run set plays but a freelance style usually dominates. Figure 2 shows a team ready to attack versus the defensive wall.

The International Handball Federation (IHF), the international governing body of team handball, has established the official rules of the game. Appendix A provides simplified rules in a handout format. You can purchase the current official *IHF Rules of the Game* from the United States Team Handball Federation, One Olympic Plaza, Colorado Springs, CO 80909.

Preparing Your Body for Success

Physical fitness alone cannot make you a great team handball player, but without it you cannot achieve your potential. Being physically fit for team handball includes endurance (aerobic and anaerobic), strength, flexibility, and the related skill factors of agility, balance, and coordination. Team handball is a 60-minute game of fast, continuous action. Your commitment to being physically fit improves your capacity to practice at a level closer to gamelike conditions. Although you may run more than 3 miles during a game, short bursts of exertion challenge your anaerobic endurance. Training your aerobic capacity through long-distance running prepares you for the short-distance speed work that will improve your anaerobic endurance for practices and games. Whenever possible, include team handball in your physical conditioning exercises. Combining skill training and fitness training in a single exercise maximizes the use of your practice time.

Every practice and game should include a 10- to 15-minute warm-up period to elevate your heart rate and increase your flexibility. The benefit of flexibility exercises increases when preceded by exercises that allow you to break a sweat. Remember to use a static stretch by assuming the stretch position, holding that position, then relaxing. Warming up decreases the chance of sustaining muscle and joint injuries.

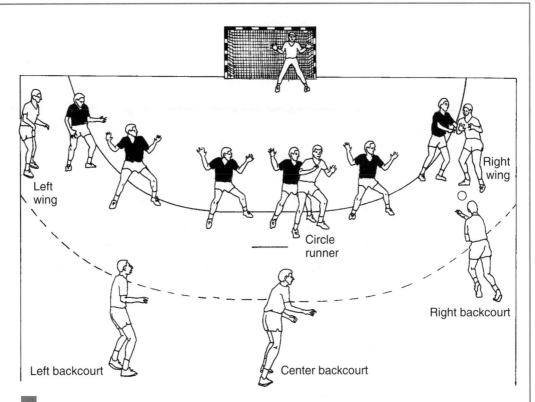

Left wing

Right wing

Circle runner

Right backcourt

Left backcourt

Center backcourt

Figure 2 Offense preparing to attack a defensive wall.

When you finish your workout, cool down by spending three to five minutes slowly jogging or walking to let your heart rate recover to its normal resting state. After walking, select a flexibility exercise for each major muscle group that you used in the training session. Include the hamstrings, quadriceps, calves, groin, shoulders, and back. Because the body is warm after training, stretching is much easier and helps prevent next-day soreness.

Team Handball Today

The International Handball Federation (IHF) recognizes the United States Team Handball Federation (USTHF) as the national governing body in the United States. The USTHF conducts national and international programs. The national teams frequently travel throughout the world for international competition including the World Championships, Pan American Games, and the Olympics. Schools are including this Olympic sport in their curriculum. Some high schools and middle schools have organized team handball intramurals and club teams who compete in Junior Olympics or state games tournaments. The Boys and Girls Clubs of America host the Junior Olympic Team Handball Nationals each May in Atlanta, Georgia.

On the college level, team handball is not yet offered as a championship sport. West Point and the Air Force Academy include team handball as a part of their varsity sport program and host tournaments. As part of a recent NCAA gender equity report, team handball was included as one of the eight suggested emerging women's sports. Team handball intramural competitions and sport clubs exist at many colleges.

New York, New Jersey, California, North Carolina, Oklahoma, Georgia, and Colorado have active USTHF state associations. Two other USTHF members, the Native American Sports Council and the U.S. Armed Forces Sports Council, are also prominent promoters of team handball. Organizations such as these, as well as individual clubs, host local tournaments and travel to compete in regional competitions. All USTHF teams are eligible to compete in the annual National Championships in April.

Several sports organizations have developed team handball for the disabled. Special Olympics International, a sports organization created for people with mental retardation, conducts team handball training schools for coaches and offers training and competition for athletes. Fourteen team handball teams competed in the 1995 Special Olympics World Games in New Haven, CT. The American Athletic Association for the Deaf sponsors a team for the World Deaf Games. The United States Cerebral Palsy Athletic Association hosts a yearly national tournament in Wheelchair Team Handball.

Team handball continues to grow throughout the world. The IHF comprises 136 member nations and 16 membership candidates. Approximately 12 million players compete in the sport on four continents. Although European and Asian countries still lead in team handball participation, African and Pan American countries are emerging in the sport. The future of team handball in the United States is promising. The interest created by the 1996 Olympic Games in Atlanta will be a catalyst for the further development of the sport.

For more information regarding specific team handball programs, call or write:

United States Team Handball Federation
One Olympic Plaza
Colorado Springs, CO 80909
719-578-4582

Special Olympics International
Team Handball Director
1325 G. St. NW
Suite 500
Washington, DC 20005-4709
202-628-3630

Boys and Girls Clubs of America
1230 West Peachtree St., NW
Atlanta, GA 30309
404-815-5700

American Athletic Association of the Deaf
3607 Washington Blvd.
Suite 4
Ogden, UT 84403-1737
801-393-7916 (TTY)
801-393-8710 (Voice)

International Handball Federation
P.O. Box 312
Ch-4020
Basel, Switzerland
41-61-331-50-15

U.S. Cerebral Palsy Athletic Association
Wheelchair Team Handball
200 Harrison Avenue
Newport, RI 02840
401-848-2460

Native American Sports Council
1765 South 8th St.
Suite T6
Colorado Springs, CO 80906
719-632-3188

U.S. Armed Forces Sports
Hoffman Building #1
Rm. 1456
2461 Eisenhower Ave.
Alexandria, VA 22331-0522
703-325-1843

T HE PLAYING COURT AND EQUIPMENT

B efore you get into the Steps to Success to develop your team handball skills, you need to learn a little bit about the playing court, equipment, and attire. In the United States, it is unlikely you will have access to an established team handball court, so you may need to learn how to modify your facility and the equipment immediately available to you.

The Playing Court

A regulation team handball court measures 20 meters by 40 meters. The rules require an additional safety zone outside the court lines of at least 1 meter on the sides and 2 meters on the ends. A large safety net is also advisable behind each goal. The most significant part of the playing court is the goal area, formed by the 6-meter line and nicknamed the "circle." Only the goalie is allowed to stand inside this area. Neither attacking players nor defending players may enter the goal area or step on the 6-meter goal-area line. However, the rules allow court players "air rights" over the circle. A player may jump from outside the goal area, hang in the air over the goal area, and shoot the ball before contacting the floor. Players cannot interfere with game action in any way after landing in the circle and must exit in the shortest route possible.

Figure 3 shows the playing court. Table 1 lists the specific rules that apply to the main court lines.

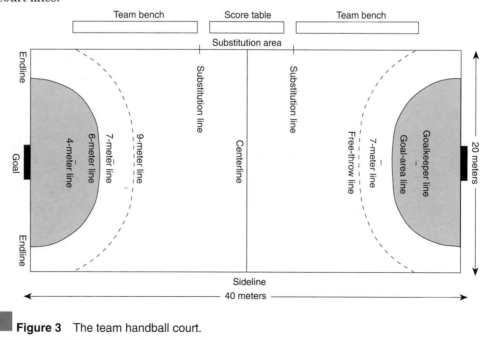

Figure 3 The team handball court.

Table 1   Main Court Lines and Restrictions
4-meter line—Goalie cannot go beyond this point on a 7-meter throw.
6-meter line—The goal-area line encloses the goal area or "circle."
7-meter line—7-meter throws are taken from this line (a penalty shot one-on-one with the goalie).
9-meter line—Free-throw line, used to put ball back into play after minor foul.
Substitution line—Marks the substitution area, a 15-centimeter line both on and off the court that designates where players enter and leave the court.
Centerline—Attacking team starts the game here and restarts play after each goal.

You may play the game indoors in the gym, outdoors on the grass, on the beach, or on any level rectangular paved area. Most high school gyms are built around a basketball court (15 meters by 28 meters) but you can easily adapt the team handball court to a smaller space. As the playing area is reduced, you may reduce the number of players, the goal-area line, and the free-throw line accordingly. Reducing the goal area when adults are playing is not recommended because it leads to an added danger for the goalie. The width of the court is more important than the length when modifying a team handball court. If putting tape on the floor is a problem, you could use the 3-point line in basketball for the goal area, but measuring the area correctly is preferable. See Appendix B for directions for marking the playing court.

The Ball

The ball consists of a rubber bladder and a white leather 32-panel cover sometimes decorated with a black symmetrical design. Considering hand size and individual strength, the ball varies in size and weight depending on the group participating (see Figure 4). To get the most out of practices, have a ball for every two players. The rules do not indicate the inflation pressure for a team handball. A simple standard is that the ball should have a good bounce when dropped from waist high, but it should not be so hard that it doesn't give a little when pressed with a thumb. Table 2 provides ball size and weight guidelines.

58-60 cm

a. Men's leather (size 3)

54-56 cm

b. Women's leather (size 2)

 **Figure 4**   The team handball varies in size and weight depending on the players.

Table 2 Team Handballs: Size and Weight		
Men's leather (size 3)	Metric	U.S. equivalent
Circumference	58-60 centimeters	23-24 inches
Weight	425-475 grams	15-17 ounces
Women's leather (size 2)		
Circumference	54-56 centimeters	21-22 inches
Weight	325-400 grams	12-14 ounces
***SuperSafe Elite** (made by Sportime 1-800-283-5700) (air-filled, foam ball for safer youth and coed training)		
6-3/4 inch handball (age 14 and older)		
Circumference	54-56 centimeters	21-22 inches
Weight	350 grams	12.3 ounces
6-1/4 inch junior handball (age 13 and younger)		
Circumference	49-50 centimeters	18-19 inches
Weight	320 grams	11.3 ounces

* Recommended for coed physical education classes and youth programs.

For beginners, physical education classes, and youth programs, the U.S. Team Handball Federation recommends the SuperSafe Elite handball by Sportime (1-800-283-5700). The air-filled, foam ball has the weight of an official women's ball (350 grams) and provides realistic play in a safe atmosphere. You can also use lighter, dense foam balls for elementary children.

The Goals

The goal has an opening of 2 meters by 3 meters with posts that are eight centimeters wide painted in a black and white checkerboard pattern (see Figure 5). The back of the goalpost is placed on the outer edge of the goal line. The net, which prevents rebounds, is 1.5 meters deep at the base of the goal. If storage might be a problem, it is important when purchasing goals to note whether you can take them apart or fold them up with ease. Fold-A-Goal (213-734-2507) sells nets and a three-piece, steel practice goal that comes apart easily, yet is durable. Field hockey or indoor soccer goals may be suitable substitutes in some situations. You can make acceptable goals of official dimensions of wood, pvc pipe, or square steel tubing. Secure them to the ground when possible. If goals are not available, tape the goal opening on a wall or make a goal with portable standards and rope. You can make net substitutes from fish netting or other sports netting and attach them with Velcro straps.

Attire

The required attire for court players is a jersey or shirt, shorts, socks, and court shoes. Many players also wear knee pads or elbow pads. Players' uniforms are numbered 1 to 20. Goalkeepers wear brightly colored long-sleeved shirts and sweat pants that distinguish them from the court players of both teams. The goalie may become a court player at any

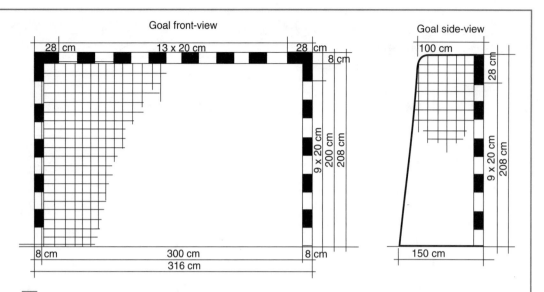

Figure 5 Dimensions of the team handball goal.

time following a change of uniform, and vice versa with court players. Referees prohibit players from wearing anything that might cause injury to another player (i.e., watch, jewelry, face mask).

Other Equipment

There are a number of other items you may want to have on hand. Here's a short list:

- First-aid kit and emergency contact numbers
- Ice and plastic bags, or a chemical cold pack
- 4-inch wide elastic wrap for compression or to hold ice pack in place
- Water
- Cones
- Mats to land on to cushion fall when learning shooting techniques
- Scrimmage vests
- Ball pump and extra needles
- Tape measure (50 meters)
- Four rolls of gymnasium floor tape (2-inch by 60-yard roll)

STEP 1

PASSING AND CATCHING: THE ESSENCE OF THE GAME

Pat Head Summitt, head basketball coach at the University of Tennessee, stresses to her basketball players the value of mastering the fundamental skills. The fundamental starting point for team handball is passing and catching. These skills always occur in combination because another player should catch and control each passed ball. As a rule, you pass with one hand so you are always a scoring threat, and you catch the ball with two hands for greater ball control. As the name team "handball" implies, using your hands to pass and catch the ball is the essence of the game.

Like basketball, there are a number of team handball passes: jump pass, bounce pass, push pass, behind the back, behind the shoulder pass, and so forth. In Step 1 you will learn two of the most frequently used passes, the overhand pass and the wrist pass. The overhand pass, which is similar to throwing a baseball, is the most fundamental passing technique. The wrist pass requires a completely different throwing action. It allows you to a make a quick lateral pass to a teammate without having to turn your body to face the receiver. You will also learn the proper techniques for catching balls above your waist, below your waist, and while you are running.

Why Are Passing and Catching Important?

Passing and catching are the most important components of ball control. Inability to control the ball results in loss of possession and increased scoring opportunities for your opponent. Offensive success revolves around a team's ability to move the ball quickly and accurately from one player to another.

When in possession of the ball your individual responsibility is to attack the goal with the intent to score. If the scoring opportunity is not clear, you must keep the rhythm of the attack going by passing the ball to a teammate. Consistent, accurate passing ensures the pace and continuity of team play and keeps pressure on the defense by allowing each attacker the opportunity to be a scoring threat.

The Overhand Pass

For two reasons, you will spend most of your practice time perfecting the overhand pass. First, because it allows you more accuracy and control, you will use the overhand pass in a game more often than any other pass. Second, if you want to be a good shooter, perfecting the overhand pass has specific importance because it lays the foundation for learning all shooting techniques.

How to Execute the Overhand Pass

The preparation phase for the overhand pass is the shooting position, which puts you in a strong posture to shoot or pass depending on the defensive situation. As you receive the pass, spread the fingers of your throwing hand comfortably across the ball and securely grip it with your fingertips. Gripping the ball properly is important for control. In preparation to pass, lift the ball up and back with your elbow flexed at about 90 degrees. Your weight should be on your back foot (same as throwing arm) and your shoulders perpendicular to the target. To make the pass, step toward your target with the foot of your nonthrowing arm. At the same time, transfer your weight from the rear to front foot, then rotate your upper body so your shoulders are square to the target. Next, lead with your elbow, whip your forearm, and finally, snap your wrist and release the ball.

A backspin on the ball while it travels through the air indicates a correct release. To follow through, let your weight rest on your front foot as your throwing arm continues in a downward, relaxed motion (see Figures 1.1a-c).

FIGURE 1.1 **KEYS TO SUCCESS**

OVERHAND PASS

a

b   c

Preparation	Execution	Follow-Through
1. Use fingertip grip ___	5. Step toward target ___	8. Bring weight forward ___
2. Flex elbow 90 degrees ___	6. Rotate and square shoulders to target ___	9. Throwing arm continues in a downward relaxed motion ___
3. Put weight on back foot ___	7. Lead with elbow ___	
4. Hold shoulders perpendicular to target ___		

The Wrist Pass

When organizing your attack in front of the defense, the wrist pass allows you to make quick passes without having to turn your upper torso in the direction of the pass. You can use your peripheral vision to see your target and follow the ball. Although the quickness of the wrist pass is an advantage, the technique limits its effective distance. You can't shoot with the ball held in this position or make a long pass with any force.

How to Execute the Wrist Pass

Face your defender with your feet shoulder-width apart, knees slightly bent, weight balanced, and holding the ball securely with both hands at waist level. To make the pass, step laterally toward the target, raise the elbow of your passing arm away from your body, and point it toward the target. At this point, your passing hand should be gripping the ball securely on top, while the other hand is supporting underneath. Now, transfer your weight toward the target, and quickly extend your elbow and forearm in the same direction. When you extend your forearm, flip your wrist in an upward motion and give the ball a final push with your thumb. Follow through naturally with your arm extended and relaxed, knee bent, and weight on your passing side foot (see Figures 1.2a-c).

FIGURE 1.2 | **KEYS TO SUCCESS**

WRIST PASS

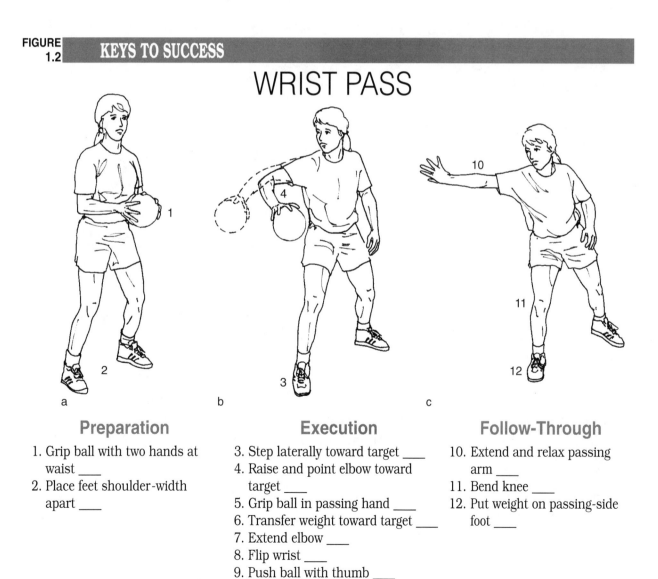

a   b   c

Preparation

1. Grip ball with two hands at waist ___
2. Place feet shoulder-width apart ___

Execution

3. Step laterally toward target ___
4. Raise and point elbow toward target ___
5. Grip ball in passing hand ___
6. Transfer weight toward target ___
7. Extend elbow ___
8. Flip wrist ___
9. Push ball with thumb ___

Follow-Through

10. Extend and relax passing arm ___
11. Bend knee ___
12. Put weight on passing-side foot ___

Catching the Ball

There are four principles that apply to catching, regardless of which technique you use. First, present a two-handed target for your teammate. Second, watch the ball. Third, extend your arms to meet the ball, and cushion its momentum by flexing your elbows as you receive it. Fourth, after catching the ball quickly prepare to shoot, fake, pass, or dribble.

How to Catch Above the Waist

When preparing to catch, align your body with the ball. Extend your arms toward the ball with elbows slightly flexed. With your fingers up and comfortably spread, form a triangle with your thumbs and forefingers, making a basket to receive the ball. As the ball arrives, flex your elbows, bringing your hands toward your chest. Grip the ball with one hand and bring it above your shoulder in preparation to shoot or pass (see Figures 1.3a-c).

FIGURE 1.3 | **KEYS TO SUCCESS**

CATCHING ABOVE THE WAIST

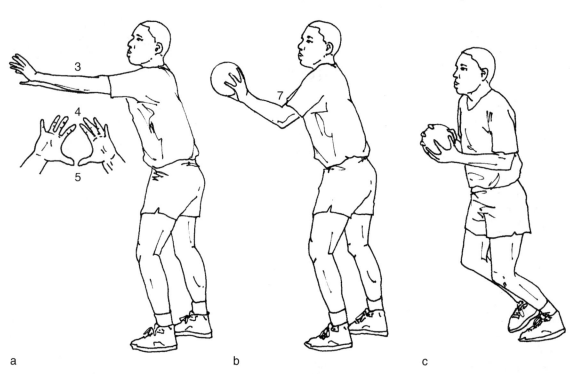

a   b   c

Preparation	Execution	Follow-Through
1. Watch the ball ___	6. Receive the ball ___	8. Bring hands to chest ___
2. Align body with the ball ___	7. Flex elbows, give with the ball ___	
3. Extend arms ___		
4. Hold fingers up ___		
5. Keep ends of thumbs almost together ___		

How to Catch Below the Waist

Of course, this is not the ideal location to receive a pass, and certainly not a place where you would give a target. But, sometimes the ball travels in unexpected ways. The best way to catch a ball below your waist is to face your palms forward and point your fingers toward the floor. Your little fingers should be almost touching so your hand position looks like a shovel. As you receive the ball, flex your elbows and bring your hands to your chest. Grip the ball with one hand and bring it above your shoulder in preparation to shoot or pass (see Figures 1.4a-c).

FIGURE 1.4   **KEYS TO SUCCESS**

CATCHING BELOW THE WAIST

a

b

c

Preparation

1. Watch the ball ___
2. Align body with ball ___
3. Face palms forward ___
4. Point fingers toward floor ___
5. Hold little fingers almost together ___
6. Bend knees ___
7. Extend arms ___

Execution

8. Receive the ball ___
9. Flex elbows, give with the ball ___

Follow-Through

10. Bring hands and ball to chest ___

How to Catch While Running

When running, it's important to catch the ball without breaking the rhythm of your movement. Push off from one leg and extend both arms toward the ball. Catch the ball and, while the other foot lands, bring the ball close to the body (see Figures 1.5a-c). When the ball comes from the side, alter this motion slightly as you turn your body sideways to catch.

1.5

KEYS TO SUCCESS

CATCHING WHILE RUNNING

a

b

c

Preparation	Execution	Follow-Through
1. Maintain running rhythm ___	4. Catch the ball ___	5. Land on other foot ___
2. Push off one leg ___		6. Bring ball to body ___
3. Extend arms toward ball ___		

PASSING AND CATCHING SUCCESS STOPPERS

Most errors in passing and catching are due to incorrect technique or misjudging speed. When passing you may misjudge the speed of a moving player, or when catching you may misjudge the speed and direction of the ball. The most common errors players make when passing and catching are listed below along with suggested methods to correct them.

ERROR	CORRECTION
Overhand Pass	
1. Your pass lacks sufficient velocity or pace.	1. The pass should be direct, snappy, and easy to catch—not too hard, not too soft, and not too slow. Pass the ball with backspin by snapping your wrist.
2. Your pass lacks accuracy.	2. Concentrate on the target. Before releasing the ball, make sure you flex your elbow about 90 degrees. Emphasize the snapping of your wrist and the follow-through.
3. Your pass goes behind a moving receiver.	3. Consider the receiver's direction and speed, and pass the ball out in front of this area. Giving a lead pass allows your teammate to be moving forward for an attack on the goal.
Wrist Pass	
1. The ball falls out of your hand as you pass.	1. Work on your grip strength and the flexibility between your fingers for increased reach (see Drills 1 and 2).
2. Your pass floats toward the receiver.	2. Step and transfer your weight toward the target. Make your elbow and wrist action quick and snappy.
3. You are facing the receiver when the pass is made.	3. Face forward, usually facing the goal and your defender, and pass the ball laterally to your teammate.
Catching	
1. The ball goes through your hands.	1. Give the passer a two-handed target and *watch the ball.* Form a basket to receive the ball by making a triangle with your thumbs and forefingers.
2. The ball rebounds off your hands.	2. Give with the ball as you catch it. Flex your elbows and gently squeeze the ball with your fingertips.

PASSING AND CATCHING

DRILLS

Gripping the ball securely is essential to maintaining control of the ball when passing and catching.

Do the first two drills daily to increase your grip strength.

1. Ball Drop

Place one hand on top of ball, spread your fingers apart, and grip the ball with your fingertips. Drop the ball and try to catch it with one hand using only your fingertips before the ball hits the floor. Do the drill with your right and your left hand.

Success Goal = 20 of 25 balls caught before they hit the floor for each hand ___

Success Check
• Fingertip grip ___
• Fingers spread ___

To Increase Difficulty
• Increase the repetitions by increments of five.

To Decrease Difficulty
• Don't drop the ball but grip it with maximum strength for 5 seconds, alternating hands.

2. Hand Tug of War

The ball is like the rope in a tug of war contest. Face your partner, and with the ball in the middle, each of you grasps the ball with the fingertips of one hand. When both of you are satisfied with your grip, one of you signals "go." The winner is the person who pulls the ball away from the other without losing their grip on the ball. Play 10 times on each hand.

Success Goal = 6 of 10 wins for each hand ___

Success Check
• Firm grip on ball ___

To Increase Difficulty
• Increase the number of times you play to 15 with each hand.

To Decrease Difficulty
• Decrease the number of times you play to 5 with each hand.

3. Ball Handling and Catching Drills

Catching is naturally practiced with passing. The following drills will help you practice your ball handling skills, check for the correct hand position when catching above and below the waist, and catch the ball on the move.

a. Move the ball around your head, shoulders, waist, and knees in one direction, then reverse direction.

b. Move the ball around your legs in a "figure 8" pattern.

c. Holding the ball with two hands at waist level, throw the ball against the floor just hard enough for it to bounce back into both hands. To check for correct hand position, hold the ball the way you caught it and check to see if your thumbs and forefingers form a triangle on top of the ball. This hand position is correct for catching balls thrown above the waist.

d. From a standing position, toss the ball with two hands above your head. As the ball falls below your shoulders, catch it with two hands. To check for correct hand position, hold the ball the way you caught it and check to see if your little fingers are almost touching and your thumbs are up. This hand position is correct for catching balls thrown below the waist.

e. Stand about 2-3 meters from a wall. Throw the ball hard against the wall and catch the rebound in the air. Varying the placement of the throw against the wall will force you to practice different hand positioning while catching the ball.

f. The purpose of this drill is to practice catching balls thrown above and below the waist. Face your partner 3 meters apart. Have your partner toss the ball randomly above and below your waist. Choose the correct hand position for catching each tossed ball.

Success Goal =

a. move ball 10 times in each direction ___
b. move ball 10 times in a "figure 8" pattern ___
c. 10 catches with correct form ___
d. 10 catches with correct form ___
e. catch 10 balls off the wall ___
f. 20 catches with correct form ___

Success Check

- Catching Above the Waist:
  Thumbs and forefingers form a triangle ___
- Catching Below the Waist:
  Little fingers almost touching ___
  Thumbs up ___
- Catching Above or Below the Waist:
  Give a two-hand target, ready to react ___
  Partner makes tosses catchable ___

To Increase Difficulty

- Face your partner and continuously pass and catch the ball while slowly running forward and backward between the sideline, always maintaining a distance of 4-5 meters between you. Your partner moves backward and rolls the ball on the ground to you while you are moving forward. Catch the ball, return it to your partner with an overhand pass, and continue toward the sideline. Switch roles and return to the opposite sideline.
- Facing your partner, continuously pass the ball with straight, lobbed, and bounced overhand passes while gradually moving apart from a distance of 4-5 meters to a distance of 15-20 meters and then approaching each other again.

To Decrease Difficulty

- Partner throws 10 passes in a row above the waist, then 10 below the waist.

4. Wall Passing

a. Practice the overhand pass technique by taping a target 1-meter square at approximately shoulder height on the wall. Position yourself 4 to 6 meters from the wall; face the wall as if facing a teammate and pass to the target. Allow the rebound to bounce, catch it with both hands, assume the ready position for the overhand pass, and pass to the target again.

b. Stand 3 or 4 meters from the wall in the ready position for the wrist pass. Your shoulders should be perpendicular to the wall. Make a wrist pass straight to the target, as if passing the ball laterally to a teammate. Allow the rebound to bounce, catch it with both hands, and assume the wrist pass ready position to pass again.

Success Goal =

a. 25 wrist passes using correct form as shown in Figure 1.1 on page 10___
   20 of 25 passes hit the target___
b. 25 overhand passes with correct form as shown in Figure 1.1___
   20 of 25 passes hit the target___

Success Check

- Wrist Pass:
  Stand perpendicular to the wall ___
  Push with your thumb ___
- Overhand Pass:
  Concentrate on correct passing form ___
  Keep eye on target ___

To Increase Difficulty

- Increase the passing distance.
- Reduce the target size to 1/2-meter.
- Stand closer to the wall and don't let ball bounce.

To Decrease Difficulty

- Eliminate the wall target.

5. Partner Passing

To practice the combined skills of overhand passing and catching, stand 4 meters from your partner. Form a two-handed target in front of your throwing hand shoulder. Pass to each other using the overhand pass. Your partner should not have to move hands from the shoulder area to catch the ball.

Success Goal = 20 of 25 overhand passes

hit your partner's target ___

Success Check

- Hands form a target ___
- Correct overhand pass technique ___

To Increase Difficulty

- Facing your partner, stand 4-5 meters from another pair of partners. Each pair has a ball. Your partner passes you the ball while you and a member of the other pair move around each other in a "figure 8" path.

6. Circle Drill

This drill gives you the opportunity to practice the overhand pass and wrist pass in a controlled space. You can practice all directions of passes in the circle formation. Form a group of five, and position yourselves evenly around a circle 10 meters in diameter. Pass the ball in any direction, across the circle or to the player standing next to you. Keep your feet moving when not in possession of the ball. Be ready to receive a pass by always showing a two-hand target to the passer. Execute correct footwork and upper body position when performing either pass. Give wrist passes to the players next to you and overhand passes to the players across from you (see Figure a).

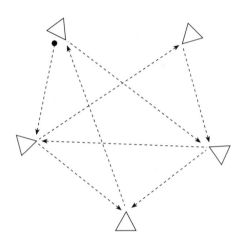

a. Overhand pass and wrist pass in any direction

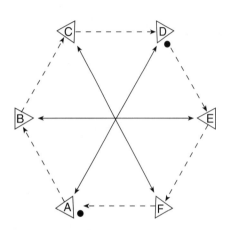

b. TO INCREASE DIFFICULTY: Passing in a hexagon

Success Goal = 45 of 50 balls accurately passed and received by the group ___

Success Check
• Be ready for the next pass ___
• Wrist pass = face forward, pass laterally ___
• Overhand pass = pass across circle ___

To Increase Difficulty
• After you pass the ball, follow your pass and run to take the place of the player that received your pass. The receiver passes to another person and runs after the pass to the new receiver's position, and so on.
• Add a player and another ball and form a hexagon. Player A passes to player B, then player A runs to position D. At the same time player D passes to player E and runs to position A. Player B passes to player C and runs to position E, and so on (see Figure b).

7. Running Partner Passing

This drill will help improve your passing and catching skills while moving down the court. Start with your partner on the goal line about 5 meters apart. Pass overhand to each other while running down the court. When you receive the ball, take three steps and pass back to your partner. Show two hands (as a target) to your partner and bring the ball to the overhand pass position quickly. The footprints shown in the figure signify taking three steps before passing back to your partner. Be sure to make a lead pass to compensate for your partner's speed and forward movement.

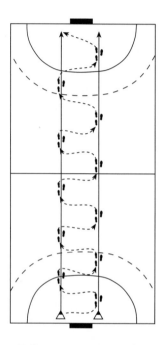

Full court partner passing

Success Goal = 10 of 12 overhand passes completed while running down the court ___

Success Check
• Use a leading overhand pass ___
• Keep running same speed down the court ___
• ONLY three steps when running with the ball ___

To Increase Difficulty
• Increase the distance between you and your partner.

To Decrease Difficulty
• Start the drill by walking down the court with your partner. Progress by increasing your speed to jogging and then running.

8. 4-Corner Drill

The purpose of this drill is to practice the overhand pass diagonally while you and your teammates are running. Position yourself and eight teammates equally in the corners of a 15-meter square. You, player A, start the drill in counterclockwise direction by making a lead pass to player B, who is running to the next corner. After passing to player B, run to the end of the line in front of you. After receiving the pass, player B takes three steps and makes a lead pass to player C, who is running to the next corner. Player C should wait until player B has *caught the ball before starting to run* . After passing, player B runs to the end of the line in front of him or her. Player C catches the ball, takes three steps, and passes to Player D, and so on. For maximum control of your passing, it's important to take your three steps properly and to step toward the target with your nonthrowing-hand foot. Continue the drill for 3 minutes or when you complete 10 consecutive passes, whichever comes first.

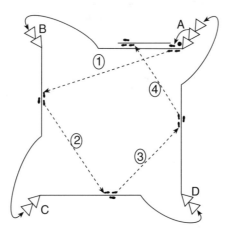

Success Goal = 10 consecutive completed passes running counterclockwise ___, clockwise ___

Success Check
• Use lead passes to moving players ___
• Catch ball running forward ___

To Increase Difficulty
• Incrementally increase the size of the square up to 20 meters.
• Add a second ball, starting it at the opposite corner of the square.

To Decrease Difficulty
• Make your square smaller.

9. Endline Handball

This game is similar to keep-away and will help you practice passing and catching in a gamelike situation. Choose two teams of equal number. Pick a playing area with a line at each end; it does not have to be a regulation court. The size of the area will vary depending on the number of players. Flip a coin to determine which team will have the ball first. After taking a throw-off at center court, the attackers attempt to move up the floor by passing ahead to an open teammate. Attackers are allowed three steps with the ball. Dribbling is *not* permitted. The defensive team matches up player to player and attempts to intercept the ball or cause a turnover. If the defense recovers the ball in such a manner, play immediately resumes in the opposite direction. Also, if the attacking team fumbles the ball and it contacts the ground, it is turned over to the defensive team and play continues from that spot. Individual defense should be played with no contact, such as in basketball. Crossing the designated line at the end of the playing area with the ball in hand scores 1 point—this includes passing to a teammate who is across the endline. Restart play after every score with a throw-off. Remember, it is a turnover if you stand and hold the ball for more than 3 seconds (see Appendix A for a review of team handball rules).

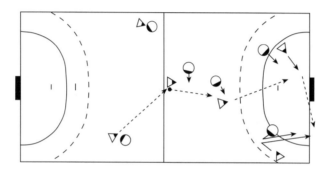

Success Goal = Your team scores a minimum of 5 points in a 5-minute game ____

**Success Check**
- No dribbling allowed ____
- Use short, quick passes versus long passes ____
- Use lead passes to moving players ____

PASSING AND CATCHING SUCCESS SUMMARY

Someone observing your passing and catching skills should focus on the specific aspects of your performance, as well as your overall movements. Passing and catching are the essence of the game. To move to more advanced individual skills and be successful in executing tactics, passing and catching must become second nature to you. You should look comfortable and relaxed as you perform the skills, not stiff or robot-like. Ask your coach or a trained partner to observe your overhand pass, wrist pass, and catching techniques. The observer can use the checklists in Figures 1.1 through 1.5 to evaluate your performance and provide corrective feedback.

PISTON MOVEMENT AND SIDE STEPPING: INDIVIDUAL ATTACK MOVES

S tagnation spells trouble for team handball attack. Just as a car will sputter and drag when all cylinders are not firing, so will your team if all six players are not moving and firing in sync. Attackers should always be in motion, making every effort to be a scoring threat and support teammates. Step 2 addresses individual movement in attack, which depends largely on the position you play. The fundamental movement of backcourt players is the piston movement, and the fundamental movement of circle runners is side stepping. Wings, depending on the situation, use both movements.

Why Are Piston Movement and Side Stepping Important?

You must master the piston movement to be an effective backcourt or wing player. The piston movement permits you to make full use of your position's depth and keep constant pressure on the defense. The wings' use of the piston movement is limited to 1 to 3 meters due to their position near the sideline. This is quite restrictive when compared to the spacious area available to the backcourts (see Figure 2.1).

Side stepping allows you to use your position's width when playing circle runner or wing. As a circle runner, you play at the 6-meter line with your back to the goal, so there is no space or tactical reason to use the piston movement (see Figure 2.1). You primarily move sideways along the 6-meter line looking for openings to receive a pass and shoot or opportunities to set picks for the backcourts. When playing

wing, you should constantly adjust your position up and down the sideline. This action helps support the backcourt in two ways: (1) moves the wing defender, creating more space for the backcourt to attack, and (2) creates open passing lanes.

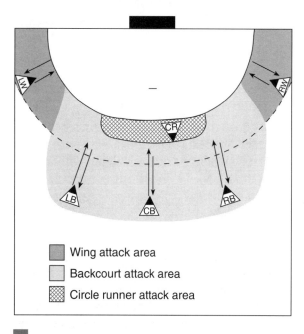

Wing attack area
Backcourt attack area
Circle runner attack area

Figure 2.1 Attack areas by position.

The Three Actions of the Piston Movement

Similar to the rapid up and down movement of a piston in a cylinder, the piston movement is the sum of three actions: (1) *run to receive*, being in motion before catching the ball, (2) *use three steps,* effective movement after you catch the ball, and (3) *back up quickly,* prepare to attack again.

Run to Receive

Being in motion before receiving the ball enhances your ability to attack in three ways:

1. It puts you in a position to support a teammate by creating a passing lane for that player to get you the ball. It also gives your teammate an indication of the direction you want to go; this will allow your teammate to give you a lead pass so you can carry out your attack without hesitation.

2. It puts you in a position to be a scoring threat. Always direct your movement toward the goal before receiving the ball. If you move toward the goal you are a potential threat to score, which keeps constant pressure on the defense. Running laterally to the goal is nonproductive movement because you are not a scoring threat and the defense will not have to respond. Being a threat to score also enhances the effectiveness of team attack. If you are occupying the attention of one or more defenders, you will disrupt the defense and your teammates will have more space to maneuver and get open for a shot.

3. It gives you an advantage as a shooter over your defender. Being in motion allows you to release the ball more quickly, which puts pressure on your defender to react. Also, the momentum created by your movement will help increase the power in your shot.

Three Steps

Team handball rules allow you to take a maximum of three steps with the ball. Failure to effectively use three steps stifles your individual creativity and disrupts the flow of the game. Taking more than three steps, or traveling, is a turnover and a free-throw for the opponent.

While executing three steps, moving the ball into the shooting position is important. This shows that you are a serious scoring threat and draws the attention of defenders and the goalie. If no shot is available, you are in an excellent position to pass to a teammate so your team's attack can continue.

Back Up, Prepare to Attack Again

If a shot is not possible after attacking and you pass the ball, it's important that you back up quickly in preparation to attack again. This action creates space between you and the defense, allowing you more freedom of movement. Remember, the ball moves quickly and your teammates rely on your support. The faster you can back up and get yourself in a position to attack, the better you can support your teammates and continue to be a threat to score.

How to Execute the Piston Movement

Effective individual movement begins with a good starting position. Place your feet shoulder-width apart with your nonthrowing-arm foot slightly out in front. Distribute your weight evenly and bend your knees comfortably. Bend your arms loosely next to your torso and keep your hands open and ready to catch the ball. Hold your head high, always keeping visual contact with your opponents, your teammates, and the ball.

As you run to receive, show a target at shoulder level that will allow you to move the ball into shooting position quickly. After catching the ball your footwork is important. If you are right handed, your three steps will be left—right—left. Step forward on your left foot, then on the second step to your right foot. Begin turning your shoulders perpendicular to the goal and bring the ball up and back. All your weight is now on your right foot, ready to transfer forward on the third step to your left foot. This stance puts you in a position to shoot or pass as you transfer your weight forward on the third step. If no shot is possible, pass the ball and back up to prepare to attack again (see Figures 2.2a-c). If you are left handed, the footwork is step right, step left, step right.

FIGURE
2.2 **KEYS TO SUCCESS**

THE PISTON MOVEMENT

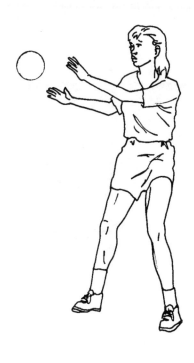

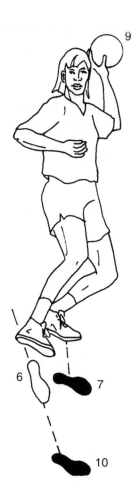

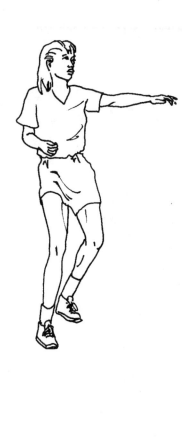

a   b   c

Preparation

1. Place feet shoulder-width apart ___
2. Bend knees comfortably ___
3. Run to receive ___
4. Hands open, ready to catch ___
5. Catch ball ___

Execution

6. Step forward on your nonthrowing-hand foot (first step) ___
7. Step with throwing-hand foot (second step) ___
8. Begin turning shoulders perpendicular to goal ___
9. Raise ball up and back (shooting position) ___
10. Step forward on nonthrowing-hand foot (third step) ___

Follow-Through

11. Pass ball ___
12. Back up quickly ___

How to Execute Side Stepping

Starting from the same position as the piston movement, step sideways with the leg on the same side as the direction you want to move. Push off a little with your other leg. As you step keep your foot close to the floor, executing a quick, flat jump sideways without crossing your feet. As you contact the floor, bring your push-off leg into balanced position. Always be ready to catch the ball. When playing circle runner, you deal with a lot of body contact that disrupts the smooth flow of your movement. To maintain a balanced position while side stepping, bend your knees to lower your center of gravity (see Figures 2.3a-c).

FIGURE 2.3 **KEYS TO SUCCESS**

SIDE STEPPING

a   b   c

Preparation

1. Place feet shoulder-width apart ___
2. Hold hands open, ready to catch ___
3. Bend knees ___

Execution

4. Step sideways ___
5. Push with opposite leg ___

Follow-Through

6. Maintain a balanced position ___
7. Catch the ball ___

PISTON MOVEMENT AND SIDE-STEPPING SUCCESS STOPPERS

The most common errors of individual movement in attack are listed here, along with suggestions to correct them.

ERROR	CORRECTION
Piston Movement	
1. You stand in one spot to receive a pass.	1. Teammates throw lead passes. You must be running to receive the pass.
2. You forget to back up after you attack.	2. You must back up quickly to prepare to attack again. Backing up also puts you in a position to receive an open pass from your teammate.
3. You catch and pass the ball while you are backing up.	3. Catch the ball moving forward. Pass to your teammate after you take your third forward step with the ball.
4. As you pass, you step forward with your throwing-arm foot.	4. Like any other throwing sport, as you throw the ball you will make a counterbalancing action by stepping with the foot *opposite* your throwing arm. You will also transfer weight from back foot to front foot.
Side Stepping	
1. You keep your hands down at your sides.	1. Keep your hands open and ready to catch the ball.
2. You stand up too straight.	2. Distribute your weight evenly and bend your knees comfortably.
3. Moving sideways, you cross your feet.	3. Maintain a balanced position.

PISTON MOVEMENT AND SIDE STEPPING
DRILLS

1. Partners Pass and Back Up

The purpose of this drill is to help you learn the sequence of the piston movement in a controlled environment.

Position yourself with a partner 5 meters from two other teammates. You (A) begin the drill by running three steps and pass overhand to teammate (C), who is directly across from you and running to receive your pass. Immediately after passing, sprint backward behind your partner (B) (see Figure a). B runs to receive the next pass from C, passes to D, then backs up quickly behind you. C and D are also alternating and performing in the same manner (see Figure b). Concentrate on backing up quickly, changing direction, and sprinting forward to receive the next pass.

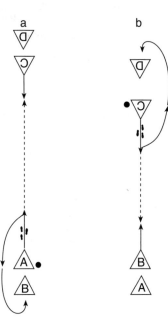

Success Goal = 30 seconds using the piston movement and passing and catching without an error ____

Success Check
• Run to receive ____
• Three-step attack ____
• Back up quickly ____

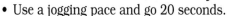

To Increase Difficulty
• Increase drill time to 1 minute.
• Alternate passing right handed and left handed.

To Decrease Difficulty
• Use a jogging pace and go 20 seconds.

2. Triangle Drill

The purpose of this drill is to help you practice the timing of the piston movement in relation to your teammates' actions. It simulates your position in the backcourt and helps you learn to pass diagonally while moving forward. It is also a great drill to improve your ball-handling skills.

Select two teammates to participate in this drill with you. Form a triangle with three cones about 5 meters apart. Each player stands in front of a cone. Face the center of the triangle and imagine a goalie directly in front of you. You (A) start with the ball, self toss, run to receive, and attack toward the center of the triangle using three steps. Do not attack directly toward your teammate. Pass to teammate (B) on your right using the overhand pass, and back up quickly to your cone. B runs to receive your pass, attacks toward the center of the triangle, passes to C, backs up to the cone, and so on (see Figure a). Make sure to keep your feet moving even when you do not have the ball. Move your feet and the ball as quickly as possible for 30 seconds, go slowly for 30 seconds, then return to maximum speed for another 30 seconds.

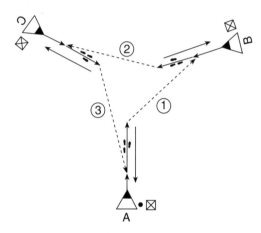

a. Piston movement in triangle formation

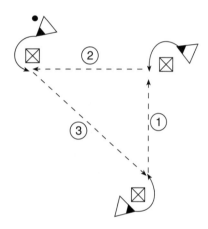

b. TO INCREASE DIFFICULTY:
Move forward in a semicircle

Success Goal = 30 seconds clockwise, rest, 30 seconds counterclockwise without dropping a pass ____

Success Check
• Hands ready ____
• Back up to cone ____
• Keep feet moving ____

To Increase Difficulty
• Increase by 10-second increments up to 60 seconds.
• Repeat the drill using your opposite hand (nondominant).
• Move forward in a semicircle around the cone (see Figure b).

To Decrease Difficulty
• Use a slower pace for 20 seconds.

3. Backcourt Piston Movement

This drill simulates the gamelike movements of the three backcourt players. You will develop the piston movement in combination with performing the overhand pass in a lateral direction. Work with six players in this drill. From two groups of three, form two horizontal lines about 6 meters apart and 3 meters between each player in the line. You will be directly across from another player. Start the ball on one end. Imagine that you are a backcourt attacking the goal then passing laterally to your teammate, and imagine that the player across from you is the goalie. Attack toward that player, then make a lead pass to the player next to you, and back up to your starting position. Always keep your feet moving, running in place, to prepare for your next attack when the ball returns to you. Move the ball in both directions.

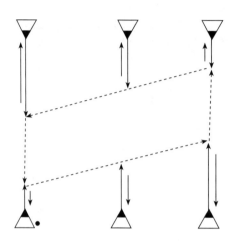

Success Goal = 45 seconds using the piston movement without dropping a pass ___

Success Check
• Run to receive in good timing with passer ___
• Accurate lead passes ___
• Keep your feet moving ___

To Increase Difficulty
• Use two balls. Start each ball at opposing ends of each line.
• Continue two-ball drill for 30 seconds without error. Increase up to 60 seconds.
• Add up to six players and four balls.

To Decrease Difficulty
• If you have a problem with lateral passing, start with the same drill formation but kneel on one knee with your nonthrowing-hand foot facing forward. Use overhand passing in the same pattern. As you prepare to pass the ball rotate your upper body so that your shoulders are perpendicular to the player across from you.

4. Circle Runner Side-Stepping Drill

The purpose of this drill is to practice the circle runner side-stepping technique while passing and catching the ball. Place four cones 7 meters from the goal about 1 meter apart. Starting next to a cone, continuously move in both directions using side-stepping steps around the cones while passing and catching a ball from a partner standing about 10 meters from the goal. Use a quick basketball chest pass to return the ball to your partner.

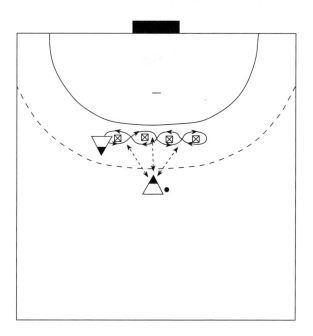

Success Goal = Player with the most passes in 30 seconds wins ___

Success Check
• Don't cross your feet ___
• Hands open and ready to catch ___
• Catch and pass quickly ___

To Increase Difficulty
• Replace cones with three semiactive defensive players. Place three players in the backcourt positions who continuously pass the ball in the piston movement against the three defenders. As a circle runner, use side steps to follow the path of the ball, move among the defenders, and position yourself to catch a pass from the backcourt players.

To Decrease Difficulty
• Don't use the cones. Use side-stepping steps in both directions in front of the 6-meter line.

5. Backcourt Movement Versus Defense

This drill simulates the gamelike movements of the backcourt players against semiactive defenders. You practice the piston movement with the added complication of defenders. Work with nine players in this drill. Form three rows of players in the backcourt positions that face three semiactive defenders standing in front of the 6-meter line. Start the ball on one end. Defenders step out toward the attackers as they catch the ball. Attack to either side of the defensive player. Make a lead pass to the player moving forward next to you, then back up to the end of your line. Move the ball in both directions.

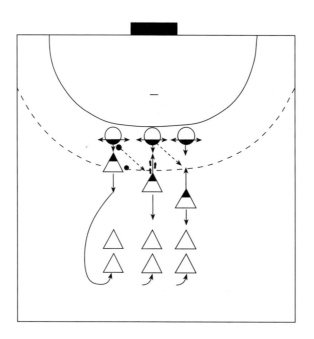

Success Goal = 60 seconds using the piston movement without dropping a pass ____

Success Check
• Run to receive in good timing with passer ____
• Attack to either side of defender ____
• Avoid contact with defender ____

To Increase Difficulty
• Increase the tempo of the piston movement.

To Decrease Difficulty
• Replace defenders with cones.

PISTON MOVEMENT AND SIDE-STEPPING SUCCESS SUMMARY

The piston movement and side stepping are fundamental to your individual movement in attack. Your effectiveness as an attacker depends to a great extent on how well you move with and without the ball. Remember, the piston movement is the sum of three basic actions: (1) *run to receive*, being in motion before catching the ball, (2) *use three steps*, effective movement after you have caught the ball, and (3) *back up, prepare to attack again*. As a backcourt and wing, standing in one position to receive the ball hinders your individual attack and stifles team attack. Proper use of the piston movement makes you a serious scoring threat, allows you to support your teammates' attacks, and helps you create space for you to attack again. As a circle runner, good side-stepping technique allows you to make use of the width of the court creating problems for the defense. As a wing, side stepping promotes effective play in your restricted space and allows you to support your backcourt. Ask your coach or trained partner to observe you practicing the piston movement and side stepping. The observer can use the checklists in Figures 2.2 and 2.3 to evaluate your performance and provide corrective feedback.

STEP 3
DRIBBLING: WHEN AND WHEN NOT TO DRIBBLE

Because of American's strong background in basketball, beginners tend to dribble too much when learning team handball. Consequently, they don't experience the dynamics of this fast-paced passing game. Dribbling should be among the skills of team handball players, emphasizing its appropriate use. Step 3 will cover dribble technique and when to use the dribble: fast-break, one-on-one, and avoiding a 3-second violation.

Why Is Dribbling Important?

Dribbling can be an asset if you use it to create scoring opportunities for yourself or teammates. Excessive dribbling serves no useful purpose. Inappropriate dribbling will destroy the game's fast tempo and the vital teamwork necessary for successful attack. Using the combination of three steps and passing is the most effective way to generate offense. However, there are three situations in which choosing to dribble will enhance your mobility and effectiveness:

1. When you have possession of the ball on a fast-break with no teammate to pass to and no defender between you and the goal, dribble to continue for a shot on goal.

2. If you have used your three steps in a one-on-one situation to successfully fake a defender, then see an open space to the goal, one dribble will permit you an additional three steps to continue to the goal for a shot.

3. When you are unable to pass to a teammate, dribbling will allow you to avoid a 3-second violation resulting in a free-throw for the opponent.

Team handball and basketball dribbling rules are the same except for two areas. First, in team handball you can take three steps or 3 seconds before and after dribbling (i.e., the steps cycle, see Figure 3.1).

The maximum movement allowed with the ball:

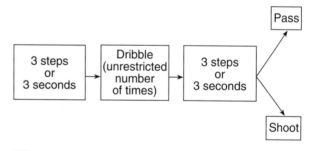

Figure 3.1 The "steps cycle."

Second, your hand must be open and on top of the ball when making contact. Palming the ball to direct it to either side, as well as double dribble, are violations resulting in free-throws. If you are a basketball player and accustomed to a larger ball, the second requirement may cause you some frustration when you attempt to dribble behind your back or try a crossover dribble.

How to Execute the Dribble

Control the ball with one open hand on top of the ball and extend your elbow to push the ball to the floor. When you extend your elbow, slightly snap your wrist and let your fingertips direct the ball in front of you. Receive the rebound with one open hand. For control, absorb the ball as it rises by flexing your elbow and hyperextending your wrist. Push the ball back to the floor by extending your elbow and snapping your wrist. Repeat these actions as many times as you need to dribble. Keep your head up so you can see the position of the goalie and the defense. This will allow you to take advantage of any opportunity to shoot or pass to an open teammate (see Figures 3.2a-c).

FIGURE 3.2 KEYS TO SUCCESS

DRIBBLING

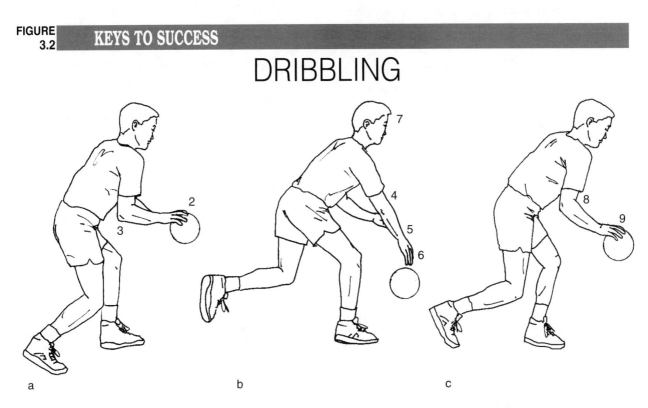

a   b   c

Preparation

1. Make the decision to use the dribble ___
2. Use open hand on top of the ball ___
3. Flex elbow at approximately 90 degrees ___

Execution

4. Extend elbow ___
5. Slightly snap the wrist ___
6. Fingertips direct the ball to the floor ___
7. Keep head up ___

Follow-Through

8. Flex elbow and hyperextend wrist as the ball rises ___
9. Use open hand on top of the ball ___
10. Extend elbow for another dribble ___

DRIBBLING SUCCESS STOPPERS

As a carryover from basketball, you may naturally dribble too much. Remember, the ball moves faster by passing to a teammate. Know when to use the dribble effectively. Also, keep your hand on top of the ball. If you use all your basketball dribbling skills, you will illegally palm the ball.

ERROR	CORRECTION
1. You dribble when passing would be more effective.	1. Dribble when you are alone on a fast-break, in a one-on-one situation, and when you are unable to pass to a teammate. Keep your head up so you can see an open teammate.
2. You are called for palming the ball.	2. Keep your hand on top of ball.
3. You are called for double dribble.	3. Remember, three steps, dribble, three steps, then pass or shoot. The double dribble violation is the same as in basketball.
4. You lose control of ball.	4. Keep dribble at waist level and push ball out in front.

DRIBBLING

DRILLS

You will usually learn and practice dribbling in conjunction with work on other skills such as passing and catching, faking, and shooting. Dribbling should not be overemphasized in the learning process, because it may lead to overuse in the game.

1. Half-Court Dribble

Can you list the three situations when using the dribble is advantageous?

1.

2.

3.

This drill will help you develop the ability to dribble full speed when all alone on a fast-break. When you are running down court in possession of the ball with no teammate to pass to and no defender between you and the goal, dribbling will allow you to continue for a shot on goal. Start on the endline and dribble full speed to center court (20 meters). Rest 20 seconds and return to endline. Work on controlling the ball by keeping it waist high and pushing it in front of you.

Success Goal = 5 full-speed trips half-court ___

Success Check

- Hold hand on top of ball ___
- Push ball in front ___
- Control ball waist high ___

To Increase Difficulty

- Use both your right hand and left hand.
- Increase the dribbling distance to the free-throw line (9 meters) on the other end and have teammates join you in the drill. You and two teammates stand in single file on one endline, and three other teammates stand opposite you on the other endline. Do the drill like a relay. You begin by dribbling down the court; when you reach the 9-meter line, pick up the ball, use three steps, and pass to a teammate who takes off in the other direction. Continue the drill until all players complete five turns with the ball.

To Decrease Difficulty

- Walk or jog and dribble half-court. This could be part of a warm-up.
- Increase rest period between your full-speed half-court trips.

2. Dribble Freeze Tag

This drill emphasizes dribble control and space awareness. The practice of continuous dribbling will help you avoid a three-second violation if you can't find an open teammate. Play this game with five teammates dribbling their own balls. Use the goal area as the playing area. You start as the chaser and try to tag your teammates while keeping control of your dribble. Any player you tag must freeze and continue to dribble in place. Players who go out of the goal area are automatically tagged and must freeze in place. Continue until every player is tagged or for 60 seconds, whichever comes first. Choose another player to be "it" and continue the game until all players have been the chaser.

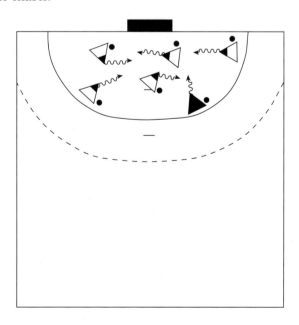

Success Goal = 5 players tagged in 60 seconds ____

Success Check
- Hold hand on top of ball ____
- Keep ball below waist ____
- Be aware of boundaries ____

To Increase Difficulty
- All players take a ball and run around dribbling within the goal area. While you are moving you must keep control of your own ball and at the same time try to knock other players' balls out of control. If you lose the ball, get it back quickly and continue to play. Work on using your body to protect the ball. Do the drill for 60 seconds.

To Decrease Difficulty
- Do not have a chaser. Players dribble and move slowly in the goal area for 30 seconds, then 30 seconds as fast as they can under control. Repeat.

3. Steps Cycle Drill

This drill teaches you how to gain an additional three steps to continue your attack. Learning this skill will increase your options to beat your opponent when in a one-on-one situation. Select five teammates to perform this drill with you. Form two equal lines 15 meters apart and facing each other. Start with a forward self toss, run to receive, take three steps, dribble once, run three more steps, and pass to the player across from you who is running to receive your pass. Follow your pass and sprint to the end of the opposite line. The player that received your pass repeats the steps cycle skill, passes, and sprints to the end of the opposite line. You may need to experiment to determine the correct footwork for each trial. Take your second set of three steps so that you throw off the correct foot (nonthrowing-hand foot forward). Continue the shuttle until each player has done the skill 10 times.

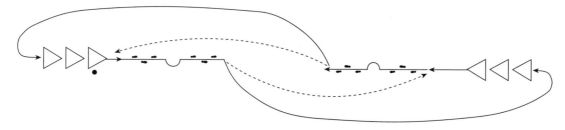

Take 3 steps, dribble, 3 steps, then pass

Success Goal = 8 out of 10 steps cycles performed correctly followed by an accurate pass ___

Success Check

• Three steps, one dribble, three steps ___
• Last step on foot opposite throwing hand ___

To Increase Difficulty

• Use a faking motion with your first three steps.
• Use a faking motion with your first three steps and fake a jump shot. Push the ball to the floor while still in the air, pick up the dribble as you come down, continue for three steps, then pass to your teammate.

To Decrease Difficulty

• Start from a stationary position and do the drill walking or jogging.

4. Dribble Relay

This drill combines the skills of passing, catching, and dribbling under the pressure of time. Work with two teams of three players each in this drill. Measuring from the wall, mark a line or place cones to represent the 6-meter line. Tape a 1-meter square target on the wall in front of each line. Each team forms a line 15 to 20 meters from the wall. The first player on each team dribbles to the 6-meter line, shoots at the wall target, retrieves the rebound of the shot, and dribbles back to the next player in line. The first team to have each player hit the target three times wins the relay. Remember to pass and shoot with your feet in a counterbalanced position. If you are right handed your left foot will be forward, and if you are left handed your right foot will be forward.

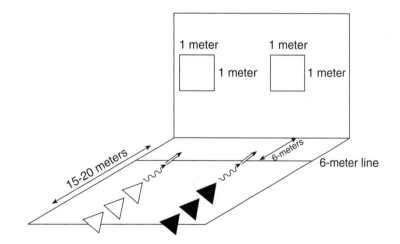

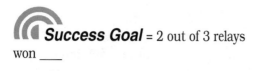

Success Goal = 2 out of 3 relays won ___

✔**Success Check**
• Control the dribble ___
• Use three steps before passing ___

To Increase Difficulty
• Start 20 meters from the wall and shoot from 9 meters away from the wall (free-throw line).
• Decrease the target size on the wall.

To Decrease Difficulty
• Do not use a target on the wall. Each player completes three turns.

5. Full Court: 3 vs. 3

This drill will help you learn how to make good decisions regarding when to dribble, pass, or use the steps cycle.

You and two teammates form a team and play team handball on the full court against three other teammates. Start with your team in attack and place yourselves along the 6-meter line. The other team must be outside the 9-meter line and ready to defend. Place one teammate in each goal area to be passers (goalie). After catching a short pass from your goalie, your team tries to beat the defenders down the court for a shot attempt from the 6-meter line. Play "make it take it" for 10 minutes and have your coach referee. The team with the most goals at the end of the playing period is the winner.

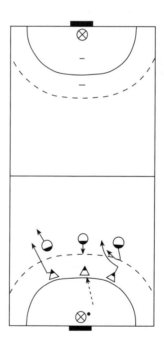

Success Goal = Team with most goals wins

Your team's score ____

Opponent's score ____

Success Check

• Avoid double dribble ____
• Use steps cycle effectively ____

To Increase Difficulty

• Place a ball by one of the goalposts of both goals. After attempting to block a shot on goal, the goalie ignores the ball that was shot and immediately picks up the ball next to the goalpost and passes to a player on his or her team. Each player should move down court as quickly as possible. All team members must be across half-court for a shot on goal to count. Continue this drill nonstop for 2-3 minutes then switch teams.

To Decrease Difficulty

• Eliminate one defender and play 3 vs. 2.

DRIBBLING SUCCESS SUMMARY

Because of the freedom of the three-step rule, you don't need to dribble to advance with the ball. Even though dribbling will allow you unlimited advancement with the ball, its inappropriate use slows down and interrupts team play. The combined use of three steps and passing is the most effective way to move the ball in attack. Dribbling should be among your skills as a team handball player, but you should learn its appropriate uses. Choosing to dribble will enhance your mobility and effectiveness in three situations:

1. When all alone on a fast-break
2. In a one-on-one situation after you have used three steps
3. To avoid a three-second violation when you cannot find an open teammate

Ask your coach or trained partner to rate your dribbling technique by using the checklist items in Keys to Success Figure 3.2. In scrimmage situations, ask your observer to evaluate your dribbling decision to see if your choices match any of three situations listed.

STEP
4 SHOOTING: FINISHING THE ATTACK

What do John Elway, Wayne Gretzky, and Michael Jordan bring to mind? Scoring. These are athletes who are always a threat to score. The objective of offense, in any game, is to score. You can have the most well-tuned offensive system and look pretty doing it, but it is of no value if you can't finish with a touchdown, or goal, or basket. In team handball, shooting is the final action in an attack—the payoff punch. There are four basic handball shots, each with its own technique, advantages, and uses. The "set shot" is the most natural of all shooting actions and is simply the overhand pass thrown hard. The "jump shot" is the most used shot in handball. Developing the ability to jump and shoot over the defense, as well as jumping inside the goal area, will make you a more effective scoring threat. The "wing shot" is the jump shot performed at a difficult shooting angle. Finally, the "fall shot" is the basic technique of the circle runner. It allows you to receive the ball on the 6-meter line and shoot without using three steps.

Why Is Shooting Important?

The fast pace of team handball provides many scoring opportunities. You must be able to choose and execute the appropriate shot as the opportunities present themselves. No matter what position you play, there are a few universal rules that apply to shooting. Your efficiency and effectiveness as a shooter depends on your knowledge and understanding of the following principles.

Principles of Shooting

1. *Shoot on the move.* This is one example of why the piston movement is so important. Shooting on the move creates momentum that gives you an advantage over the defense, allowing you to deliver the shot more quickly and powerfully. Keep in mind that running into a defender who has established proper position is the same as "charging" in basketball and is a foul resulting in a free-throw.

2. *Watch the goalie* and shoot at an area of the goal that the goalie is not covering. Remember, not only must you beat your defender but the goalie also.

3. Shooting the ball hard is not enough to beat a good goalie; *accuracy* is essential. Shoot for the corners. The high corner "cobwebs" are under the crossbar and inside the goalpost. The low cobwebs are where the goalposts meet the floor, above where the goalie's foot can extend and below where the goalie's hand can reach (see Figure 4.1). When shooting low, you may choose

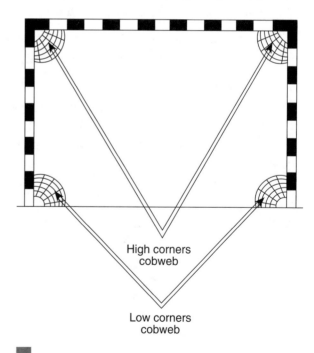

High corners
cobweb

Low corners
cobweb

Figure 4.1 Shoot for the cobwebs.

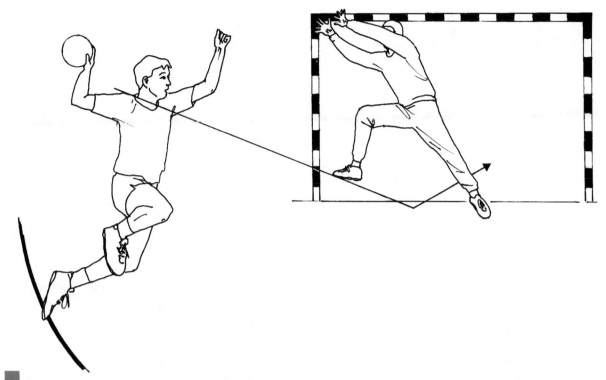

Figure 4.2 Bounce shot under the goalie.

to shoot a "bounce shot." Even though a direct shot is quicker and more accurate, the bounce shot changes the speed and direction of the ball, making it more difficult for the goalie to stop (see Figure 4.2).

4. *Consider your distance and angle to the goal.* When learning to play there is a natural tendency to shoot from anywhere at every opportunity. Although it is important for a shooter to possess an aggressive mentality, you have to be smart about some things (see Figure 4.3).

You should know your limitations as a shooter, particularly when it comes to deciding how far out you should take a shot. You may be accurate, but if you can't get enough velocity on the ball the goalie will have more time to react and block your shot. Most shots are taken in the area between the 6-meter and 9-meter lines. Be aware that even though you may be close to the goal, shooting from an extreme angle makes the goalie's job easier and your job harder. The more severe the shooting angle, the less open goal space there is for you to shoot at, reducing the space the goalie has to cover (see Figure 4.4).

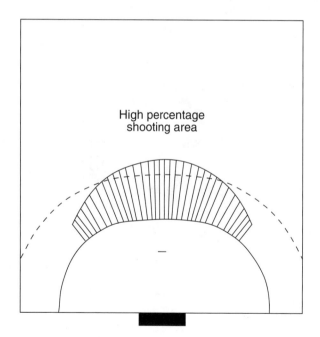

Figure 4.3 Highest percentage shooting area based on distance and angle to goal.

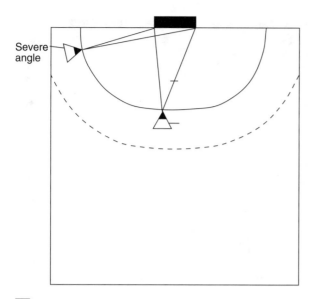

Figure 4.4 Sharp-angle shots are usually not successful.

5. *Shoot when there is an opening*, over defenders, around defenders, or between defenders. If there is a clear path, you can run between defenders and jump into the goal area to shoot (see Figure 4.5). To be an effective shooter a key phrase to

Figure 4.5 Running between defenders and jumping into the goal area to shoot.

remember is "do not force your shot." Attempting to shoot when there is no opening stifles the attack and constitutes dangerous play. According to the rules, an offensive player cannot carelessly shoot a ball that hits a stationary defender or even fake a threatening throw to an opponent's face. Endangering your opponent in such ways will likely result in a 2-minute suspension.

How to Execute the Set Shot

The mechanics of the set shot are the same as the overhand pass, only the player throws the ball hard with the intent to score. It is the overhand pass in exaggerated form, like a center fielder trying to throw someone out at the plate.

For the set shot to be effective you must perform it quickly. This requires a minimum time from catching the ball to shooting it. *Preparation* is the key. "Run to receive" to get into shooting position. The momentum created from being in motion will increase the power of your shot. Upon receiving the pass, use the "three steps" and on the second step quickly bring the ball up to head height or higher. Extend your arm back comfortably and flex your elbow to 90 degrees or greater. At this point, all of your weight is on your back foot. Keep your upper body upright, your shoulders perpendicular to the goal, and your head up with the goal and goalkeeper in your field of vision. This position will help you protect the ball from the defense and allow you to shoot at any moment. To shoot, step forward and transfer your weight from your rear to your front foot. Rotate and open your shoulders so they are parallel to the goal. Begin moving your arm forward by leading with your elbow, then whip your forearm and snap your wrist. To follow through, allow the momentum of your body to continue forward and the motion of your throwing arm to continue across your body (see Figures 4.6a-c).

FIGURE
4.6

KEYS TO SUCCESS

THE SET SHOT

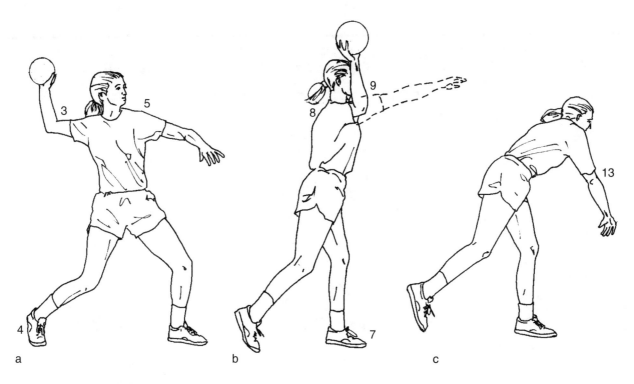

a   b   c

Preparation

1. Run to receive ____
2. Attack using three steps ____
3. Flex elbow to 90 degrees ____
4. Put weight on back foot (same as throwing arm) ____
5. Hold shoulders perpendicular to goal ____
6. Keep head up and eyes on goalie ____

Execution

7. Step forward—transfer weight from rear foot to front foot ____
8. Rotate and square shoulders to the goal ____
9. Lead with elbow ____
10. Whip forearm ____
11. Snap wrist ____

Follow-Through

12. Momentum is going forward ____
13. Throwing arm motion continues across body ____

How to Execute the Jump Shot

Use the jump shot to shoot over the defense and to penetrate the goal area. The throwing action of the jump shot is basically the same as the set shot, only you perform it while jumping.

First, run to receive, then use three steps to gain momentum for your jump. Take a long diagonal third step, planting your foot and flexing your knee to help you change some forward momentum into vertical.

This last step is important because it provides the upward force for maximum height in your jump. Assist your jump by driving up the knee of your nonjumping leg. As you explode off the floor, lift your opposite arm slightly in front of your body for balance and rotate your shoulders perpendicular to the goal. Stretch your shooting arm back as far as is comfortable, and hold the ball above your head. Keep your head up and eyes focused on the goal and the goalie. Now you are ready to deliver the shot quickly and forcefully at the top of your jump. Swing your nonthrowing arm toward the rear and rotate your shoulders to face the goal. Move your throwing arm forward by leading with your elbow, whipping your forearm, and snapping your wrist. As you are throwing, pike slightly at your waist to help generate maximum power. Completely follow through by allowing your body's momentum to continue forward, the motion of your throwing arm to continue across your body, and by landing on your jumping leg (see Figures 4.7a-c).

FIGURE 4.7 **KEYS TO SUCCESS**

THE JUMP SHOT

Preparation

1. Run to receive ___
2. Use three steps ___
3. To jump, plant foot in the last step (opposite foot of the throwing arm) and drive other knee up ___
4. Bring shooting arm up and back ___
5. Bring nonshooting arm slightly in front of your body ___
6. Hold shoulders perpendicular to the goal with head up ___

Execution

7. Swing nonshooting arm toward rear ___
8. Rotate shoulders ___
9. Whip throwing arm forward (elbow, shoulder, forearm, wrist) ___
10. Pike slightly at your waist ___

Follow-Through

11. Momentum forward ___
12. Throwing arm continues across the body ___
13. Land on take-off foot ___

The Wing Shot

Good wing players increase the effectiveness of a team's offense and scoring potential by making the full width of the court useful. Learning the wing shot technique will allow you to turn what would be a low-percentage scoring opportunity into an excellent one. There is one cardinal rule that you must adhere to when playing the wing: NEVER SHOOT A SET SHOT. To have a chance at scoring, you must jump inside the goal area to increase your shooting angle. So, the wing shot is much like the jump shot with a few modifications in technique (see Figure 4.8).

How to Execute the Wing Shot

You should learn technique for the wing shot in the following progression: (1) the approach, (2) the plant, (3) the jump, and (4) the shot.

1. The approach—Be in motion to receive the ball. Your space is limited in the wing, so you probably won't be able to run forward to receive a pass. Just make sure you are in motion, feet moving in place, and ready to move forward when you get the ball. After receiving the pass, use your three steps to accelerate toward the 6-meter line. The greater your acceleration, the

more horizontal distance you can cover when jumping into the goal area. The farther you jump, the better shooting angle you can create.

2. The plant—Look for the 6-meter line to avoid stepping on it. On your third step, plant the foot opposite your shooting arm and point it roughly in the direction of the 7-meter line. At this point flex the knee of your jumping leg.

3. The jump—Hold the ball in both hands to protect it, and swing it inside the goal area. Now jump off your planted foot and drive your opposite leg forcefully forward and up. To improve your chance of scoring, you must increase your shooting angle, so all body movement should be toward the 7-meter line. At this point, your shoulders are perpendicular to the goal (see Figure 4.9a).

4. The shot—When you are in the air above the goal area, release your support hand and lift the ball up to throwing position. Focus on the goal and hold this position until you are ready to shoot. Then rotate your shoulders to face the goal, lead with your elbow, whip your forearm, and snap your wrist (see Figure 4.9b). Follow through by allowing the momentum of your body to continue forward and the motion of your throwing arm to go across your body. Land on your jumping leg (see Figure 4.9c).

Figure 4.8 Jumping inside the goal area to increase your shooting angle from the wing.

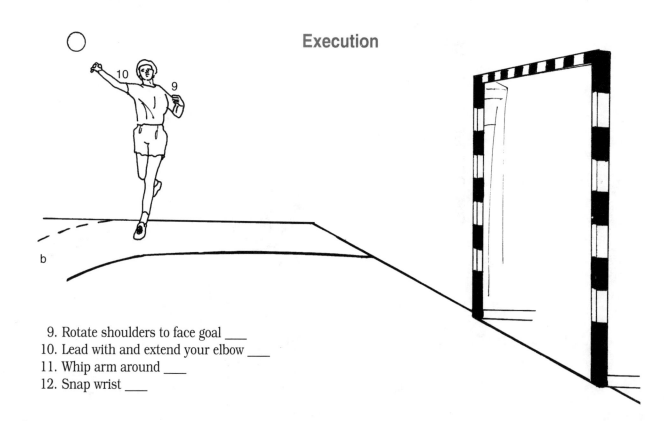

FIGURE 4.9

KEYS TO SUCCESS

WING SHOT

Preparation

1. Be in motion to receive ___
2. Use three steps (accelerate toward 6-meter line) ___
3. Plant foot opposite shooting arm ___
4. Drive shooting-arm leg forward and up ___
5. Jump toward the 7-meter line ___
6. Bring ball up into shooting position ___
7. Hold shoulders perpendicular to the goal ___
8. Head up, watch goalie ___

Execution

9. Rotate shoulders to face goal ___
10. Lead with and extend your elbow ___
11. Whip arm around ___
12. Snap wrist ___

Follow-Through

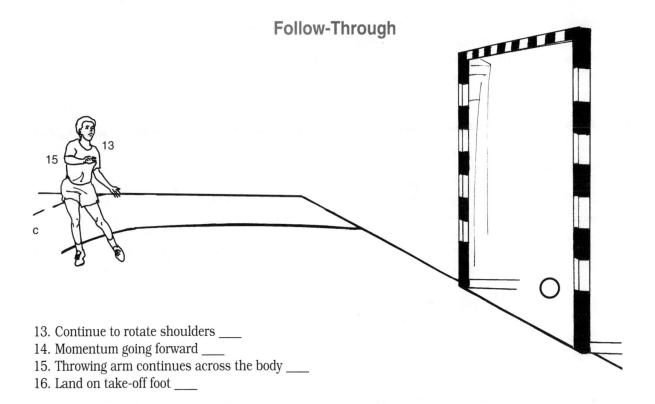

13. Continue to rotate shoulders ___
14. Momentum going forward ___
15. Throwing arm continues across the body ___
16. Land on take-off foot ___

Because of its unnatural components, your first wing shots may be wild and, consequently, dangerous for the goalie. So, it's a good idea to begin practicing wing shots without a goalkeeper. This will not only save the goalie undue stress but also give you a chance to develop accuracy without the added pressure of beating a goalie. Concentrate on learning to shoot to the long high corner and the long low corner of the goal. The bounce shot is effective to the long low corner (see Figure 4.10).

Setting the goal at a 45-degree angle will simulate the presence of a goalie and force you to shoot to the long corners (see Figure 4.11).

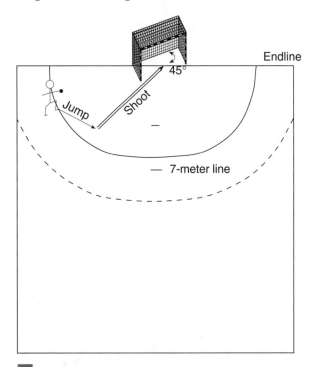

Figure 4.11 Goal at 45-degree angle—jumping toward the 7-meter line.

Figure 4.10 The long high corner and the long low corner of the goal from the left wing position.

When your accuracy and technique have improved, put the goal back on the goal line and add a goalie. The wing shot is difficult to learn and perfect, so use the progression and be patient with yourself.

The Fall Shot

The fall shot is primarily used by the circle runner, who normally receives the ball near the 6-meter line with his or her back to the goal. This position dictates that you must turn and fall into the goal area to deliver an effective shot. If you are afraid to fall you cannot master this shot. Put in extra time practicing the technique for cushioning your fall until you feel comfortable and confident.

How to Execute the Fall Shot

In the circle runner ready position, your feet are shoulder-width apart, knees flexed, upper body slightly forward, and your hands are chest high to receive a pass. After receiving the ball you must execute the shot quickly and decisively, because the defense is so concentrated on the 6-meter line. Keep both hands on the ball to protect it from the defense, pivot, swing the ball inside the circle, and lean directly toward the goal. Fall toward the goal by pushing forward with one or both legs. Keep your head up with your eyes on the goalkeeper. Release your support hand from the ball and bring your shooting arm up and back. Shoot quickly and explosively by whipping your arm forward and snapping your wrist. In the follow-through you must prepare for floor contact. Cushion your fall by extending your arms to the floor with your elbows slightly flexed, and catch yourself with your hands to absorb the shock (see Figures 4.12a-c).

FIGURE 4.12 **KEYS TO SUCCESS**

THE FALL SHOT

  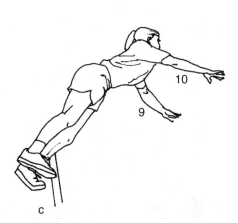

a   b   c

Preparation

1. Have back to goal ___
2. Flex knees, hold hands chest high ___
3. Pivot, swing ball inside the area ___

Execution

4. Push toward goal ___
5. Lift shooting arm up and back ___
6. Keep head up, eyes on goalie ___
7. Whip throwing arm forward ___
8. Snap wrist ___

Follow-Through

9. Extend nonthrowing arm to the floor ___
10. Extend shooting arm to the floor ___
11. Flex elbows ___
12. Catch yourself with hands ___

The 7-meter Throw

The referee awards a 7-meter throw when a foul obstructs a clear scoring opportunity. In most instances, a clear chance to score means you have gone around the defender and are shooting near the circle. There is no 7-meter shot awarded if you maintain full ball and body control when being fouled. The referee will allow you to continue for the score.

Your coach may choose any player to take the 7-meter throw. To execute the throw, you must keep one foot in contact with the floor and you cannot touch the 7-meter line. Therefore, the set shot and the fall shot are used (see Figure 4.13). Other players must be behind the 9-meter line and at least 3 meters from the ball until the shooter releases the ball. Similar to executing a free-throw in basketball, offensive players are allowed to rebound a blocked 7-meter shot and shoot at the goalie again from the 6-meter line. Play also continues if a defensive player rebounds the ball. The 7-meter throw is an important part of the game so you should practice it at every training session.

Figure 4.13   The 7-meter throw.

SHOOTING SUCCESS STOPPERS

Remember the principles of shooting for every shot you take: (1) shoot on the move, (2) watch the goalie, (3) shoot for the corners, (4) consider distance and angle of the shot, and (5) shoot when there is an opening. The most common errors for the set shot, jump shot, wing shot, and fall shot are listed here with suggestions for correcting them.

ERROR	CORRECTION
Set Shot	
1. You are standing still when you take a shot.	1. Always run to receive, use your three steps, then shoot.
2. As you take a shot, the foot on the same side as your throwing arm is your last step.	2. If you are right handed, step left, right, left (left handers step right, left, right). Make good use of your allowed three steps.
3. You shoot in the middle of the goal and hit the goalie.	3. Look at the goalie and shoot to the open corner.
4. Goalie catches your shot taken from 12 meters.	4. To take advantage of your power and accuracy, take most set shots from 9 meters to 10 meters. Do not shoot too far away.
5. You are fouled before you can release a shot.	5. Don't get too close to your defender. Try to avoid free-throws. Even though a minor foul results in a free-throw for your team, it interrupts the flow of attack and allows the defense to rest.
Fall Shot	
1. You step on the line as you pivot to shoot.	1. If you start next to the line, do not take a step with your pivot foot. Catch the ball, pivot to face the goal, fall, and shoot.
2. You release your shot standing up, then fall in the area.	2. Say to yourself, "Pivot, fall, shoot." You fall forward first and shoot on the way down.
Wing Shot	
1. You shoot a set shot from the wing and hit the goalie.	1. Jump inside the area to increase your shooting angle. Look for the long corner.
2. You receive the ball standing still.	2. Show some forward motion before receiving the ball. Your teammate will be giving you a lead pass. Space is limited in the wing so you don't have as much space to run to receive as you do in the backcourt.
3. You step on the line when shooting.	3. Look at the 6-meter line as you take off. To help condition yourself while you practice, have a teammate yell "line" if you step inside the area on your shot.

ERROR	CORRECTION
Jump Shot	
1. You are called for a charging foul when attempting to shoot a jump shot over a defender.	1. Don't take off too close to your defender. Remember you must transform your forward momentum into vertical height when shooting over defenders.
2. Your jump shot lacks velocity.	2. Concentrate on your shoulder rotation. Shoulders are perpendicular to the goal before the shot. As you shoot, the shoulder rotation adds power to your shot.
3. You feel awkward on take-off before the jump shot.	3. Run to receive and use your three steps. Your take-off leg is opposite your throwing arm. Remember, step left, right, left for right handers, and step right, left, right for left handers.

SHOOTING

DRILLS

1. Set Shot Target Practice

The purpose of this drill is to help you practice set shot technique, shooting on the move, and shooting accuracy. Use gym floor tape (five centimeters wide) to make a goal 2 meters by 3 meters on the wall. Tape targets in each corner 1 meter by 1 meter and mark a line 9 meters from the wall. Start about 12 meters from the wall and toss the ball out in front of you. This gentle toss is important because it gets you in motion to catch the ball, like run to receive. Use three steps to get into shooting position. Shoot on the move aiming for a corner.

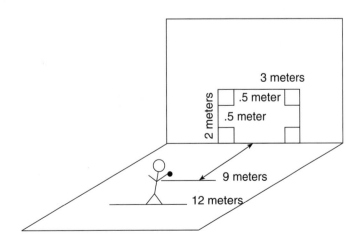

Success Goal = 6 out of 10 shots in a corner target ____

Success Check
• Toss and run to receive ____
• Three steps to shooting position ____
• Aim for a corner ____

To Increase Difficulty
• Shoot from 10 meters.
• Shoot three in a row to a corner target before moving to the next corner.

To Decrease Difficulty
• Make the corner targets bigger.
• Shoot from the 7-meter line.

2. Jump Shot Footwork

This drill is a progression designed to help you master the jump shot footwork. Examples are for a right-handed player.

a. Start about 5 meters from your partner. Stand on your right foot and throw to your partner.

b. Stand one step from a line on the floor opposite your partner, who is 6 meters from the line. Take one step on your left leg, jump over the line, and throw to your partner before landing. You step left, then jump and throw.

c. Stand three steps away from 6-meter line. Take three steps, jump over 6-meter line into goal area, hang in the air, and shoot at the goal. You step left, right, left, jump, and shoot.

d. Start about 12 meters from the goal. Toss ball slightly in front of you and run to catch it. Take three steps, jump for maximum height, hang, and shoot at the corners of the goal.

e. Stand parallel to your partner about 12 meters from the goal. Run to receive a pass from your partner at the 9-meter line: (a) catch the ball, (b) take three steps, (c) jump over the 6-meter line into the goal area, (d) hang in the air and look at the goalie, and (e) shoot the ball and score! Take turns passing and shooting with your partner. Put towel targets in the high corners and cones in the low corners of the goal if you do not have a goalie.

Success Goal = 5 to10 times for each step of the progression ____

Success Check
• Jump off your nonthrowing-hand foot ____
• Jump for maximum height____
• Hang in air, then shoot ____

3. Attack, Pass, and Shoot

This drill allows you to practice backcourt shooting in a more gamelike manner. It will help you develop the proper timing you need to play cohesively with a backcourt teammate. You will work on making a lateral lead pass to an attacking teammate and receiving a lateral lead pass in preparation to deliver a set shot or jump shot. Place targets in corners of the goal (i.e., towels, small hula hoops, hang a sheet to cover up middle of goal, cones in lower corners). With teammates, form one line in the left backcourt position and one line in the right backcourt position about 12 meters from the goal. Your coach or teammate stands in the center backcourt position as a stationary passer. Positioned in the right backcourt, you run to receive a pass from your coach, attack the goal using three steps, then pass laterally to the left backcourt. The left backcourt will be running to receive so you must give a lead pass. When the left backcourt receives the pass, the player attacks using three steps and shoots a set shot from the 9-meter line. The left backcourt and right backcourt switch lines after the shot. When everyone has shot, repeat the drill and shoot from the right backcourt. Shooters, remember to look at the goalie.

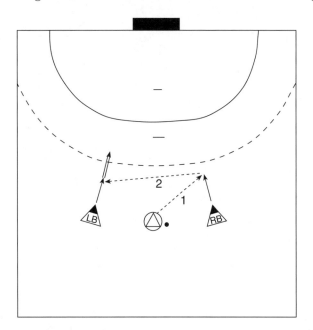

 **Success Goal** = 6 out of 10 set shots from:

    Left backcourt hitting target ___
    Right backcourt hitting target ___

Success Check

- Run to receive, attack, and pass or shoot ___
- Timing: receive ball at 11 or 12 meters ___
- Shoot from the 9-meter line ___

To Increase Difficulty

- Add a goalie and defender at 8 meters.
- Do a fake, followed by a jump shot over a defender at 8 meters.

To Decrease Difficulty

- Use no targets.

4. Jump Shot With Screen

This drill will help you learn to control your forward momentum when jump shooting over the defense. It will also help you improve your timing when working in combination with a team-mate.

Set up targets in the goal (see Drill 1). Position yourself in the left backcourt about 12 to 14 meters from the goal. Have your partner do the same in the right backcourt. The drill starts with the right backcourt running toward the 7-meter line and you passing the ball to this teammate at about 9 meters (see Figure a). After your partner catches the ball, you run toward the center of the court and receive a return pass. Use three steps to accelerate, plant, and shoot a jump shot over your partner, who is positioned at about 8 meters to serve as a screen (see Figure b).

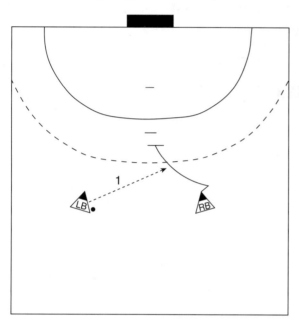

a

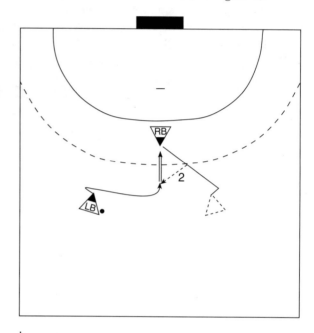

b

Success Goal = 6 out of 10 jump shots hit a target ___

Success Check
• Step left, right, left (right hander) ___
  Step right, left, right (left hander) ___
• Not too close to the screen and defense to avoid charging foul ___
• Shoot at maximum height of your jump, hang ___

To Increase Difficulty
• Add a goalie.
• Add defense with hands up to set screen on and to shoot over.

To Decrease Difficulty
• Start with ball, self toss, take three steps, and shoot a jump shot.

5. Wing Shot

The purpose of this drill is to help you get familiar with the floor space you have to work with in the wing. It also allows you to practice technique without the pressure of a goalie. Position the goal away from the goal line at a 45-degree angle. Start in the left wing position (or the right wing if you are left handed) where the 9-meter line meets the sideline. Self toss the ball slightly ahead so you will be running forward when you catch the ball. Use three steps, jump toward the 7-meter line, and shoot for the long corners.

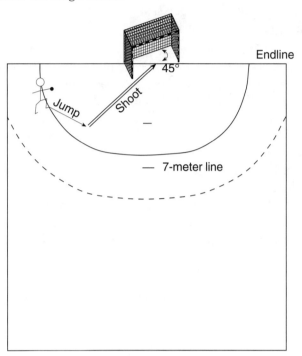

Success Goal = 6 out of 10 wing shots in a long corner ____

Success Check
- Watch the line ____
- Jump toward the 7-meter line ____
- Hang and shoot for a long corner ____

To Increase Difficulty
- Place the goal in proper position and add a goalie.
- Add a goalie and a pass from a backcourt player.
- Add a goalie, a pass from a backcourt player, and a cone on the 6-meter line that represents your defensive player. From the left wing, attack to the left of the cone and jump into the goal area toward the 7-meter line. From the right wing, attack to the right of the cone.

To Decrease Difficulty
- Use no goalie and leave the goal on the goal line.

6. Fall Shot Learning Progression

As a beginning circle runner, the fear of falling may inhibit you from learning the fall shot and eventually the more advanced dive shot. Use appropriate mat cushioning and take gradual steps in the development of this shot. Tumbling skills like the forward, backward, and shoulder rolls as well as push-ups can be used as warm ups for fall shot practice. This drill will help you safely learn the fall shot technique.

On a padded carpet or tumbling mat, position yourself across from your partner. Start about 3 meters apart and use the following progression. Do not advance to the next progression until you have successfully completed the previous one.

   a. In a push-up position, bend your arms to push your body up off the ground. Then land on your arms again, cushioning the force of the fall by bending your elbows.
   b. Kneel on both knees (you may want to use knee pads). Bring the ball up to shooting position. As you fall forward, pass the ball to your partner. Cushion your fall with both hands like a push-up position.
   c. Stand with feet shoulder-width apart. Bend knees and bring ball to shooting position. Fall forward and pass to your partner. Cushion your fall as in a.
   d. Start with your back to your partner. Pivot, fall forward, and pass the ball to your partner. Cushion your fall as in a.
   e. Repeat the same progressions on the 6-meter line in front of the goal. Start with a tumbling mat inside the goal area, then repeat without a mat. Shoot at the goal rather than passing to a partner. Remember, you can't contact the floor inside the goal area until after you release the ball.

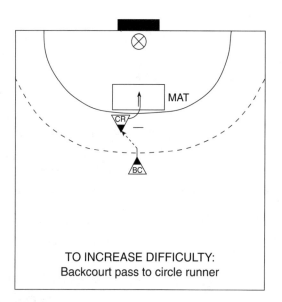

TO INCREASE DIFFICULTY:
Backcourt pass to circle runner

Success Goal **Success Goal** = 10 repetitions of each progression using the correct technique ___

Success Check **Success Check**
• Fall forward ___
• Look at partner or goal and shoot ___
• Cushion fall ___

To Increase Difficulty
• On progression e, add a goalie and a pass from the backcourt (see Figure).
• When you have successfully completed e, add a passive defender on the circle.

7. Half-Court: 3 vs. 2

The purpose of this drill is to focus on attacking and shooting with emphasis on shot selection. This situational play helps you learn to choose the best shot for a given situation. Select four teammates and a goalie to participate with you in this drill. Start a goalie in the goal and two defensive players on the 6-meter line. If you do not have a goalie, put targets in the corners of the goal. The offense begins with a circle runner, left backcourt, and center backcourt. These are your starting positions, but you may move around anywhere within the boundaries of the designated playing area. The boundaries are the boundary line shown in the figure below extending left to the sideline, forward to the endline, and back to the centerline. Now you are set to play a minigame using all the rules of team handball. The only exceptions are that the defensive players must play basketball-style defense (no contact), and your team must make at least three passes before taking a shot. Keep in mind that you are playing 3 vs. 2, so find the open player. The defense receives 2 points for any unsuccessful shot by the offense—blocked shot, goalie save, or missed shot. The offense receives 1 point for every made shot. The game ends after the fifth shot on goal, so keep score accurately. At the end of each game rotate positions clockwise. This will give each player a chance to play with different combinations of people and different positions.

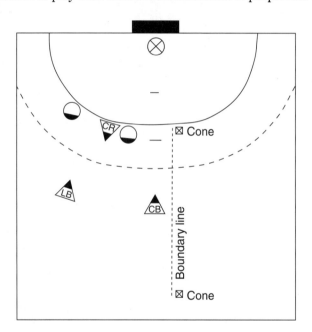

Success Goal = Your team scores more points than your opponent:

Your points ___

Opponent's points ___

Success Check

• Attack the goal; be a threat to shoot ___
• Pass to open player ___
• Use the piston movement ___

To Increase Difficulty

• Decrease the width of the playing area.
• Play 3 vs. 3—make it take it; first team to 10 goals wins.

SHOOTING SUCCESS SUMMARY

Shooting is the final action in attack, the decisive moment, the payoff punch. Learning to master the four basic shots, to select them appropriately and execute them flawlessly, might make you the Michael Jordan of team handball. You can become a player that is a threat to score at any time, under any circumstance. All it takes is a little hard work and dedication. Start slowly when learning new shooting skills. If you have not been throwing regularly, too much shooting practice will make your arm sore. It is all right to learn a skill at half speed; then, as your skill increases, increase your pace and intensity. Practicing shooting against a defender makes your performance more gamelike. Ask your coach or a trained partner to rate your technique according to the checklist items with the Keys to Success for the set shot, jump shot, wing shot, and fall shot (see Figures 4.6, 4.7, 4.9, and 4.12).

STEP

5

INDIVIDUAL DEFENSIVE SKILLS:
GOING ONE-ON-ONE

During the 1994 NBA Championships Hakeem Olajuwon said that he played team handball when growing up in his native Nigeria. When you watch him play "big man" defense, you can get a little glimpse of it coming through. The skills Olajuwon displays when he gets strong position on an opposing center, moves well to prevent him from penetrating to the basket, then blocks his shot are the same skills required to become a solid team handball defender. In this game, the attacker is always the initiator, and it is the defender's role to neutralize the attacker's actions. Step 5 will teach you the correct elements of individual defense to help you accomplish that task: (1) basic stance, (2) checking your opponent, and (3) shot blocking.

Why Are Individual Defensive Skills Important?

You've heard it said that a chain is only as strong as its weakest link. This holds true in team handball also, particularly as it applies to defense. To have a strong defensive team, the chain, takes fundamentally sound defenders, the links. Mastery of individual defensive skills will ensure your ability to neutralize your opponent's attack and to contribute your part to the team's defensive effort.

Basic Stance

Effective checking and shot blocking begin from the basic stance. In the basic defensive stance your feet should be shoulder-width apart, knees slightly bent, and weight on the balls of your feet. Keep your upper body upright with a slight lean forward at the hips. Keep your head up and use your peripheral vision to keep track of both the ball movement and your opponent's location at all times. Hold your hands up about shoulder height and slightly wider than shoulder-width apart (see Figure 5.1a). You may have to experiment a little to find a comfortable and functional stance that permits balance and mobility.

Checking—Making Contact With Your Opponent

Checking can be from a little touch to continuous body contact. The rules allow you to use your upper body to obstruct an opponent with or without the ball. To check your opponent, step forward on your leg that is on the same side as your opponent's shooting arm, and extend your hand on that side to make contact with the ball or shoulder. This will inhibit the player's ability to shoot or pass effectively. At the same time, your other hand should contact your opponent's hip (see Figure 5.1b). Applying this resistance will deter the player's forward momentum and help you feel which direction the player wants to move. Using the open hands within the confines of the upper body is a necessary defensive technique to stop your opponent. Get close enough to look like two people in a slow dance position.

Once you have established contact, continue checking with the idea of mutual resistance. This means not overpowering your opponent, but applying force equal to your opponent's attack. Move your feet to stay between your opponent and the goal, and use your leg strength to resist your opponent's forward momentum (see Figure 5.1c). Don't push your opponent out of the play. Just try to resist to the point of changing the player's forward movement to lateral movement. The key phrase to remember is "play defense with your feet."

FIGURE 5.1   KEYS TO SUCCESS

CHECKING

a

b

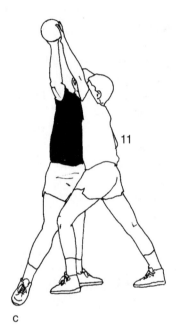

c

Preparation—Basic Stance

1. Feet shoulder width ___
2. Knees bent ___
3. Weight on balls of feet ___
4. Upper body upright, slightly forward ___
5. Eyes on opponent ___
6. Hands up ___
7. Step out to meet attacker ___

Execution

8. Your leg forward on shooting-arm side ___
9. One hand on hip ___
10. One hand on shoulder or ball ___

Follow-Through

11. Slow dance position ___
12. Maintain contact and move your feet ___

Aggressive body-to-body checking that prevents your opponent from continuing the attack is called a "tie-up" and results in a free-throw. This is most likely to occur when an attacker is attempting to drive to the 6-meter line. In such a case tying up is a good action, even though a foul is called, because it interrupts the flow of the attack and prevents a potential scoring chance (see Figure 5.2).

Figure 5.3 The punishment ladder.

How to Block Shots

Blocking is the last opportunity to prevent a shot on goal by putting your hands in the path of the ball. In a game, you will see players blocking both individually and collectively in the air and on the ground. Individual blocking is used when you are in a one-on-one situation and you have to stop your attacker by relying only on your own skills. Anytime you are unable to check the attacker you should take on a goalie's mentality, have your hands up, and make every effort to block the shot. Even if you don't block the ball, the blocking action serves as an obstruction by interfering with the shooter's vision. Blocking also takes away a portion of the goal as a shooting option, giving the goalie a better idea of where the attacker has an opening to shoot.

Figure 5.2 Tying up.

When checking an opponent, however, if you direct your actions exclusively at the opponent and not the ball you will be punished progressively: warning, 2-minute suspension, disqualification (see Figure 5.3). Basically these actions include reaching around, holding, pushing, tripping, or hitting the opponent. If these actions destroy an opponent's clear chance to score, a 7-meter throw will also be awarded.

As the ball leaves the shooter's hand, watch the ball and extend your arms fully into its path. Keep your hands open and fingers slightly spread with your thumbs almost touching. *Attack the ball aggressively.* Move your arms forward against the force of the shot and block with both hands. This not only helps you stay aggressive but also helps prevent elbow hyperextension.

Set Shot Block

To block a set shot keep your feet in contact with floor while you bend and reach to adjust your arm position to the path of the ball (see Figures 5.4a-c).

FIGURE 5.4	KEYS TO SUCCESS

SET SHOT BLOCK

a

b

Preparation—Basic Stance

1. Feet shoulder width ___
2. Knees bent___
3. Weight on balls of feet ___
4. Upper body upright, slightly forward ___
5. Eyes on opponent ___
6. Hands up ___

Execution

7. Watch the ball ___
8. Extend arms fully ___
9. Hands open, thumbs almost touching ___

c

10. Attack the ball ___

Jump Shot Block

Blocking jump shots is similar to volleyball blocking in that you must jump, reach, and attack the ball while in the air. Time your take-off so you jump just *after* the shooter jumps (see Figures 5.5a-c). Otherwise, you will be coming down when the ball is shot and have no chance to block it. Depending on the distance between you and the shooter, blocking can be done from the basic position or with a step forward. In both cases, you prepare to jump by bending your knees then pushing off forcefully with both legs. The arms should be fully extended into the path of the ball. Keep your hands close together with your palms open. If the shooter changes his or her throwing position while in mid-air, try to adapt to the change by leaning in that direction.

FIGURE
5.5

KEYS TO SUCCESS

JUMP SHOT BLOCK

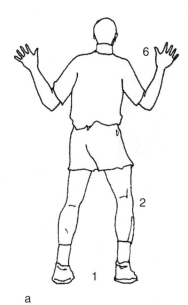

a

b

c

Preparation

1. Feet shoulder width ___
2. Knees bent ___
3. Weight on balls of feet ___
4. Upper body upright, slightly forward ___
5. Eyes on opponent ___
6. Hands up ___

Execution

7. Watch ball and shooter ___
8. Bend knees, prepare to jump ___
9. Jump *after* shooter jumps ___
10. Keep hands open ___
11. Attack the ball ___

INDIVIDUAL DEFENSIVE SKILLS SUCCESS STOPPERS

Team handball is a contact sport that requires aggressive individual defense. If you play much noncontact basketball, you may have trouble adjusting to checking your opponent. Remember to step out to meet your opponent, making contact with the hip and shooting shoulder. When blocking a shot, extend your arms into the shot's path and attack the ball. Keep in mind that blocking the jump shot requires a little timing delay compared to the attacker's jump. The most common errors in individual defense are listed here with suggestions for correcting them.

ERROR	CORRECTION
Basic Stance	
1. Similar to the basketball basic defensive stance, you bend forward at the hips with your hands out in front, palms up.	1. The team handball basic defensive stance requires your upper body to be upright with your hands up and shoulder-width apart.
Shot Blocking	
1. The ball goes through your hands as you block it.	1. Extend your arms with your hands open, fingers spread. Your thumbs are almost touching so the ball has no space to go through.
2. The shot touches your hands but the force knocks your arms back and the ball continues on its path to the goal.	2. Be aggressive and move your arms forward against the force of the shot. Attack the ball!
3. You attempt to block a jump shot but fail because you are coming down as the shooter releases the shot.	3. Time your take-off so you jump just after the shooter jumps. This is similar to blocking in volleyball.
Checking	
1. You step out but avoid contact with your opponent.	1. Effective checking requires making body contact with your opponent, like two people in a slow dance position.
2. Grabbing or pushing your opponent results in a 2-minute suspension.	2. Keep your hands open and move your feet after making contact. To avoid pushing, keep arms flexed.

INDIVIDUAL DEFENSE

DRILLS

1. Defensive Footwork

This drill will give you practice moving and changing direction in your defensive stance, helping to improve your balance and body control.

Stand about 6 meters from your partner, facing each other. Your partner holds a ball with two hands at waist level. When your partner slaps the ball with one hand, you immediately get to basic stance and begin moving your feet quickly in place. From there your partner will indicate your movement by moving the ball to different positions.

A. If your partner extends the ball in one hand to either side, shuffle to that side.

B. If your partner puts the ball in shooting position, run forward.

C. If your partner extends the ball toward you, run backward.

D. You can also do this drill with your entire team, having your coach direct.

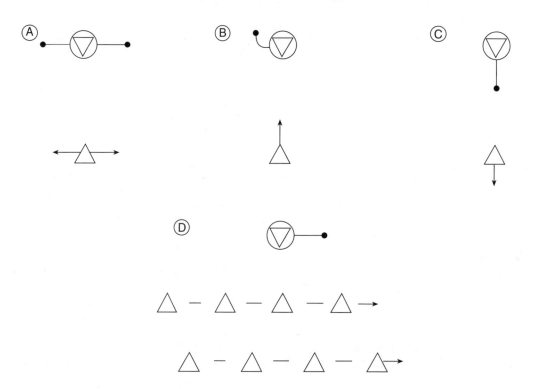

Success Goal = 20 seconds continuous movement ____

✔ Success Check
• Basic stance ____
• Shuffle, keep feet moving ____
• Step out, back up ____

To Increase Difficulty
• Change directions faster.
• Increase time by 5-second increments.

To Decrease Difficulty
• Reduce time to 10 seconds.

2. Making Contact

These drills will help you learn to maintain contact with a moving offensive player and give you good practice for defensive footwork.

a. Breaking out of the circle: Six defending players stand in a circle 2-3 meters apart with you in the middle of the circle as an attacker. Your objective is to break out of the circle while the defenders try to obstruct you by checking you, using only the torso.

b. Partner shuffle: Partners face each other standing in the basic position with knees bent. Put your hands up slightly in front of your shoulders. Place your hands flat against your partner's hands. Without losing contact, shuffle sideways the width of the court, and return to your starting point.

c. Checking in pairs: Your partner imitates a set shot as you take one step out from the basic position and make contact at the hip and shooting shoulder. Repeat this drill 15 times, then switch roles.

d. Three passes and check: You and a teammate face each other 4-5 meters apart while continuously side-stepping between the sidelines. You start with the ball and make three passes between each other. On the third pass your teammate attacks while you try to obstruct your partner by checking him or her. Make sure you make contact correctly.

Success Goal = 5 round trips without losing contact ____

Success Check
• Maintain contact ____
• Keep feet moving ____

To Increase Difficulty
• Partner shuffle: Partners take turns being the leader. For 1 minute the leader changes the pace and direction of the movement, and the follower has to react and keep up. Rest 1 minute and change leaders. If contact is broken before the 1-minute limit, note the time and change leaders. The player with the most time keeping contact wins. Play the best of five.

To Decrease Difficulty
• Slow down the pace.

3. Step Out and Check Drill

The purpose of this drill is to practice the movement of stepping out and making proper contact with an attacker. You will need two teammates to help you in this drill. Your teammates position themselves on the 9-meter line facing the goal about 2 meters apart, with one ball. Position yourself on defense at the 6-meter line between the two of them. When your teammate slaps the ball, slide along the 6-meter line until you are directly in front of your teammate. When your teammate raises the ball to shooting position, step out and check, making contact with the hip and shoulder (see Figure a). When you make contact, your teammate passes over to the other, you recover diagonally to the 6-meter line, then slide directly in front of the ball. When the ball is raised to shooting position, step out, check, and recover when the ball is passed (see Figure b). Continue the drill for 30 seconds, then rotate clockwise until everyone has been on defense.

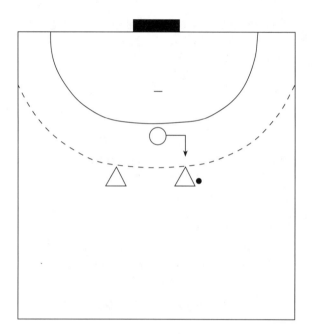

a. Step out and make contact

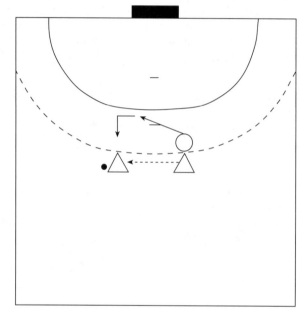

b. Recover to 6-meter line

Success Goal = 30 seconds using proper technique ___

Success Check
• Step out aggressively ___
• Contact shooter's hip and shoulder ___
• Recover diagonally to 6-meter line ___

To Increase Difficulty
• Increase by 10 second increments up to 60 seconds.

To Decrease Difficulty
• Add a second defender and decrease time to 20 seconds.

4. Partner Blocking

This drill allows you to practice blocking technique and gradually conquer any fear you might have of the ball hitting you.

Face your partner about 2 meters apart. Your partner is the shooter with a ball (if you have several balls place them on the floor beside your partner so the balls can be thrown consecutively). You are the defender. The shooter throws 10 balls, at about 50 percent speed, past you but within your reach, and you try to block the balls. The shooter tries to shoot all around you, over your head and to either side. It would be convenient to have a barrier about 6 meters behind you so you don't have to chase the balls very far.

(Wall)

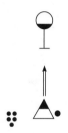

![Success Goal icon] **Success Goal** = 8 of 10 balls blocked ___

![checkmark] **Success Check**
- Watch the ball ___
- Extend arms ___
- Attack the ball ___

To Increase Difficulty
- Increase the velocity of the shot.
- Shoot jump shots.

To Decrease Difficulty
- Players move closer together, about one-half to 1 meter apart. The shooter fakes a shot and keeps control of the ball as the blocker extends to touch the ball with two hands.

5. Shot Blocking

The purpose of this drill is to improve your reaction time and aggressiveness in shot blocking. One defender stands at 7 or 8 meters in front of the goal. Five shooters line up in single file at 12 meters, each with a ball. In rapid succession, the shooters approach the defender and shoot from the 9-meter line. The defender gets 1 point for touching the ball and 2 points for a block; the defender loses 2 points for each goal allowed. Change the defender when every shooter has shot. Continue this rotation until everyone has been the defender.

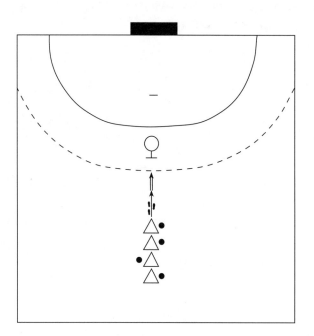

Success Goal = The winner is the player with the most points at the end of the drill ___

Success Check
• React to the shooter's attack ___
• Be aggressive ___

To Increase Difficulty
• The defender sits on the floor and, as the shooter attacks, gets up to block each shot.
• The defender retreats to the 6-meter line after each shot, then steps out to block the next.

To Decrease Difficulty
• Shoot at 50 percent velocity.

6. One-on-One

This drill allows you to practice all your individual defensive skills under gamelike conditions. Place two cones or other markers on the 6-meter line about 1 meter outside each goalpost. One defender stands on the 6-meter line directly in front of the goal. Five attackers, each with a ball, line up single file at about 12 meters. A passer, preferably a coach, stands to either side of the attackers at about 10 meters. The attacker passes to the coach and runs to receive a return pass. The defender steps out to meet the attack at the 9-meter line. All action must take place within the boundaries. The attackers can either attempt to shoot or fake and drive to the 6-meter line. The defender tries to prevent either option by checking and trying to tie up the player for a free-throw, or blocking the shot. The coach serves as referee and blows the whistle to stop play on a free-throw or out of bounds. Switch defenders every five attacks until everyone has been on defense.

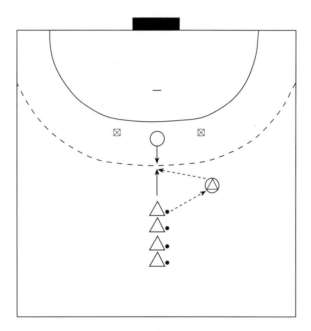

Success Goal = 3 of 5 tie-ups (free-throws) or blocked shots ____

Success Check
• Step out in good timing ____
• Maintain contact, keep feet moving ____

To Increase Difficulty
• Increase the number of attacks to 10 per defender.

To Decrease Difficulty
• Decrease the size of the boundaries.
• Designate fakes and drives only or BC shots only.

INDIVIDUAL DEFENSIVE SKILLS SUCCESS SUMMARY

Don't be a weak link; take pride in your individual defense. Like Hakeem Olajuwon, you can make an invaluable contribution to your team. Be alert, aggressive, and visually aware of all activity around you. "Play defense with your feet," be in perpetual motion. Move with short, quick shuffle steps, prepared to check an attacker or block an attacker's shot. Ask your coach or trained partner to rate your technique according to the checklist items with the Keys to Success for basic stance, checking, and shot blocking (see Figures 5.1, 5.4, and 5.5).

STEP

6 GOALKEEPING: THE COMPETITIVE EDGE

G oalkeepers in team handball have to cope with shots coming at them at speeds of up to and over 80 mph. It requires all their courage, skill, and exceptional reflexes to face these bullet-like throws and stop the ball from entering the net. The goalies are always at a disadvantage, but the best of them can point to a save rate of more than 40 percent. It often verges on magic when they succeed in the last moment in stopping the ball from crossing the goal line. Get ready to experience firsthand what it is like to be in the goal. First, learn what rules apply only to you and how to protect yourself in the goal. Next, find out how to position yourself in the goal, then block high, low, medium, and wing shots. Last, learn to quickly recover the shots you block, then initiate the fast-break. Good luck!

Why Is Goalkeeping Important?

A poor goalie can make a good team mediocre, and a good goalie can make a mediocre team competitive. Not only are you the last line of defense but also the

---

Specific Rules That Apply to Goalies

Specific rules that govern the goalkeeper:

The goalie is permitted to do the following:

- Block the ball with any part of the body while inside the goal area.
- Move around with the ball inside the goal area with no restrictions except against intentionally delaying the game.
- Leave the goal area at any time subject to the rules applied to court players.

The goalie is not permitted to do the following:

- Leave the goal area while in possession of the ball (free-throw).
- Touch the ball while it is stationary or rolling on the ground outside the goal area while standing in the goal area (free-throw).
- Re-enter the goal area from the playing area while still in possession of the ball (7-meter throw).
- Receive a pass from a court player while inside the goal area (7-meter throw).

Goal-throw is awarded for the following:

- The goalie blocks the ball and recovers it in the goal area.
- The ball goes over the endline after the goalkeeper blocks it.
- The attacking team throws the ball over the endline.

To execute the goal-throw, stand inside the goal area and throw the ball to a teammate.

If the goalie blocks a shot and the deflected ball goes out of bounds on the sideline, the attacking team keeps the ball, putting it back into play with a throw-in.

first attacker in offense because of the responsibility of beginning the fast-break. Your effectiveness greatly affects the psychological state of your teammates, and your overall performance is of considerable influence to team success. Regardless of your success or failure, you must be a leader and display the intangible qualities of confidence, composure, and courage.

How to Protect Yourself in the Goal

In team handball, the shooter intends to score a goal, not to hit the goalie. As you begin to train keep in mind, however, that most Americans are accustomed to throwing a ball directly to someone (i.e., baseball, basketball, football). This carryover from other sports and being unaccustomed to the size of a handball causes beginning shooters to be inaccurate. Consequently, many of your teammates will unintentionally shoot the ball at the goalie instead of shooting to the open corners of the goal. Ultimately, good technique will be your best protection. Until you've learned basic goalie technique and your teammates have mastered shooting the ball with reasonable accuracy, use targets in the corners of the goal for game-like drills and scrimmages.

Here are some ideas to protect your body while practicing goalie technique: To soften the ball impact, have a partner throw at you from 3 to 6 meters at a moderate to slow speed. You can use dense foam balls and partially deflated volleyballs for your beginning goalie training. Old tennis balls thrown consecutively at a moderate speed from about 4 meters will help you work on your reaction time. Protect yourself from the sting of blocking by wearing a long-sleeved shirt and long pants. Males should wear a protective cup, and many goalies also wear knee and shin pads.

How to Position Yourself in the Goal

Assume the basic stance whenever an opponent has possession of the ball within shooting distance of the goal. The stance is similar to a court player's defensive basic stance. Stand tall with your feet shoulder-width apart and knees flexed. Your weight should be slightly forward on the balls of your feet and evenly distributed. Keep your arms up and elbows bent with your hands either shoulder or waist high. You will adjust your hand position according to the type of shot and your personal preference (see Figure 6.1a).

Your movement should provide maximum protection of the goal at all times. Pay particular attention to guarding the short corners of the goal. These are the top and bottom corners closest to the attacker with the ball. Because the attacker is closer to them, the short corners are often easier targets to shoot at than other parts of the goal. For this reason it is important to stay between the attacker with the ball and the short corners. This will force him or her to take a more difficult shot, which decreases the chance of scoring.

Be aware of the entire offensive situation, but keep your eyes on the attacking player and the ball. Move laterally along an imaginary arc between the two goalposts (see Figure 6.1b). Do not move directly along the goal line. A good rule of thumb is to start in the center of the goal, one step out from the goal line. From this position, however, there is no way you can see the goalposts. You must learn to sense where you are in relation to the goal opening. Having your hands up between your shoulders and waist will help you locate the goalposts and determine your position. As the ball is passed from player to player, use short, quick shuffle steps to mirror the movement of the ball. Be ready to change direction at any time. Keep a position on the imaginary line that bisects the angle between the ball and the goalposts (see Figure 6.1c). Paying attention to the defense, the developing offensive situation, and the ball helps you anticipate when and where a shot will be taken.

FIGURE
6.1

KEYS TO SUCCESS

POSITIONING YOURSELF IN THE GOAL

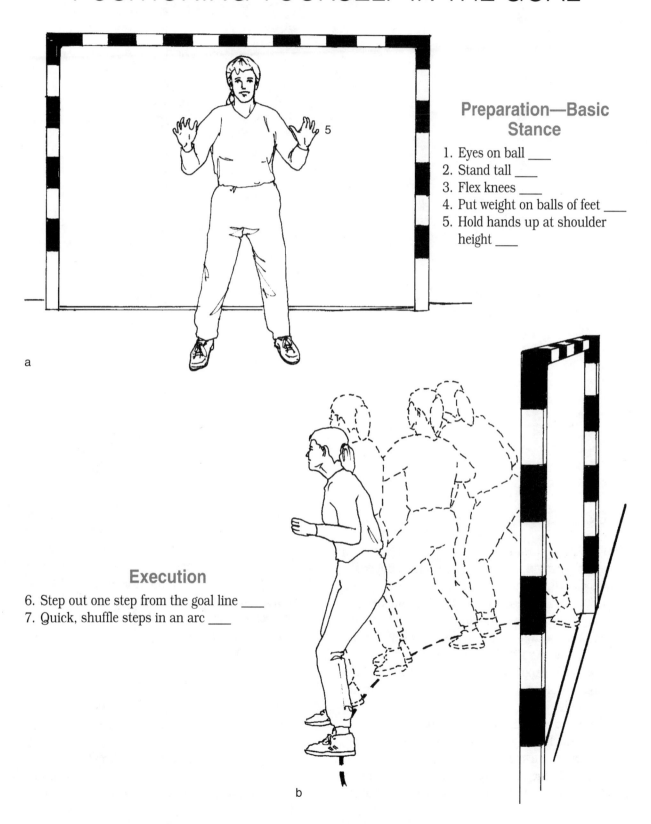

Preparation—Basic Stance

1. Eyes on ball ___
2. Stand tall ___
3. Flex knees ___
4. Put weight on balls of feet ___
5. Hold hands up at shoulder height ___

a

Execution

6. Step out one step from the goal line ___
7. Quick, shuffle steps in an arc ___

b

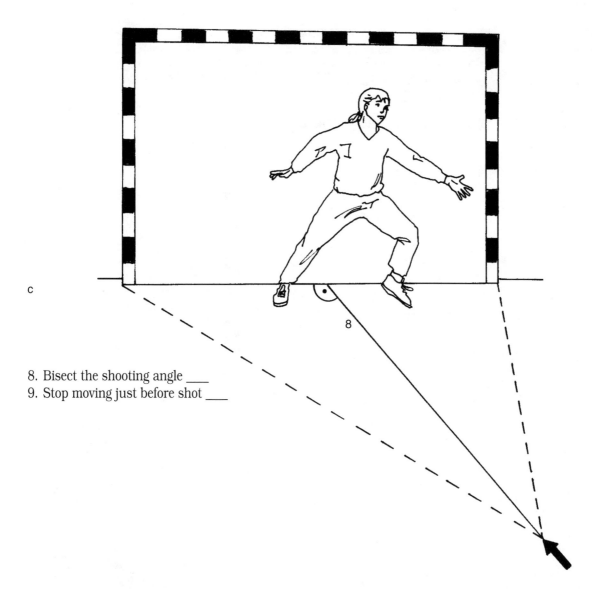

c

8. Bisect the shooting angle ___
9. Stop moving just before shot ___

Blocking Shots

Positioning yourself in the goal (review Figure 6.1a) is the preparation phase for all the shots the goalie will block. When a player is ready to deliver a shot, stop moving and get stable in the basic position. *Don't begin the blocking action until the ball is r eleased.* Moving prematurely will only assist the shooter because the shooter will shoot away from the direction in which you've moved. This timing is important and requires absolute concentration. When the shooter has committed, act quickly and decisively. As you move toward the ball, point your ball-side foot toward the sideline, trying to put as much of your body as possible in the line of the shot. Whether you block the ball with one or two hands will depend on how much time you have to react to the shot. Don't make the mistake of trying to catch the ball. Concentrate on making the block, then trying to gain control of the ball as quickly as possible. Avoid diving for the ball because it takes too much time to regain your footing. This extra time will put your team at a disadvantage in transition because you will not be able to recover the ball quickly. Being on the floor will also put you at a disadvantage if the opposition fields the rebound for another shot.

How to Block High Shots

To block high shots, stand tall, keeping your center of gravity as high as possible, and take a small step in the direction of the shot (see Figure 6.2a). Push off the leg farther from the ball and leap in the direction of the shot, simultaneously extending your arm(s) into the path of the ball (see Figures 6.2b and c).

FIGURE 6.2

KEYS TO SUCCESS

BLOCKING HIGH SHOTS
Preparation

a

1. Stand tall ___
2. Take step in ball's direction ___

Execution

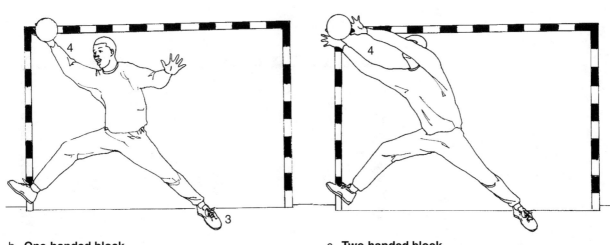

b. **One-handed block**

3. Push off and leap toward shot ___
4. Extend arm(s) in path of ball ___

c. **Two-handed block**

5. Attack the ball ___

How to Block Low Shots

To block low shots, keep your center of gravity low and take a small step in the direction of the shot. Push off the leg farther from the ball in the direction of the shot (see Figure 6.3a). Attempt to block the shot by extending both your leg and arm into the path of the ball. Lift and shoot your leg out into the path of the ball. Then cover the space above your leg with your arm moving in a downward arcing motion. Remember this key phrase: "Shoot and cover" (see Figure 6.3b).

FIGURE 6.3	KEYS TO SUCCESS

BLOCKING LOW SHOTS
Preparation

a

1. Take a small step in direction of the ball ___
2. Push off leg farther from ball ___

Execution

b

3. Lift knee ___
4. Shoot leg ___
5. Extend arm and cover with hand ___
6. Attack the ball ___

How to Block Medium High Shots

To block medium high shots means to block balls coming between the shoulder and knee level. These shots cause some difficulty because they are in the in-between area of blocking with your arm and leg. Generally, block medium high shots by using your hand and leg. Starting from the basic position, take a small step in the direction of the ball, raise your knee, and lower the hand closest to the shot. The leg farther from the ball pushes the body in the direction of the shot, then with a little hop, helps to maintain body balance on one foot. Attempt to cover as much area as possible when moving your leg and hand into the path of the ball. When attempting the block, the distance of the shot from the body determines the degree of bend in the arm and leg. The opposite hand moves upward to help maintain your balance (see Figure 6.4).

FIGURE 6.4

KEYS TO SUCCESS

BLOCKING MEDIUM HIGH SHOTS

1. Take a small step in direction of the ball ___
2. Lift knee and lower hand into path of the ball ___
3. Push off in direction of the ball ___
4. Maintain body balance on one foot ___
5. Extend leg and hand into the ball's path ___
6. Attack the ball ___

How to Block Wing Shots

On shots from the wings, it is important to protect the short corners of the goal and force the shooter to shoot for the more difficult long corners. Stay close to the goalpost, with your arm on the goalpost side held up with the forearm protecting your face. Your other hand is placed out to the side bent at about 90 degrees. Most of your weight should be on your goalpost-side foot (see Figure 6.5a). When the shooter jumps into the area, take one step out from the goalpost and move with short steps to cover the shooter's angle. As the shot is taken, stop moving and focus on the ball (see Figure 6.5b). Attempt to block low, medium, and high shots using the proper technique (review Figures 6.2, 6.3, and 6.4; see Figure 6.5c).

FIGURE 6.5 — **KEYS TO SUCCESS**

BLOCKING WING SHOTS

a

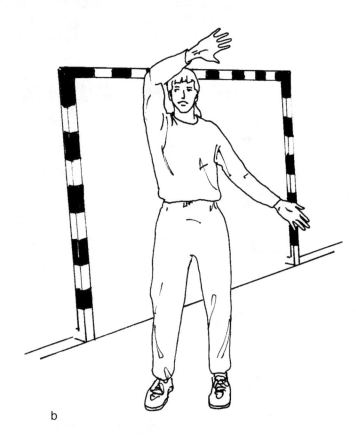

b

Preparation

1. Stand tall close to the goalpost ___
2. Goalpost-side arm up, forearm protecting face ___
3. Keep free hand out to side, bent about 90 degrees ___
4. Put weight on goalpost-side leg ___

Execution

5. Take one step out as shooter jumps ___
6. Take short steps to cover shooter's angle ___
7. Stop moving, eyes on ball ___

c

8. Push off goalpost leg toward path of ball ___
9. Block the shot ___

Recovering the Ball and Initiating the Fast-Break

The actions of recovering the ball and initiating the fast-break follow every ball you block. Your effectiveness as a goalkeeper is not only judged by your ability to block shots but by how quickly you can re-cover the ball and put it back in play. The speed, precision, and judgment with which you perform this skill set the pace for the entire attack. To initiate the fast-break, you must be equally skilled in the short outlet pass and the long "touchdown" pass to a breaking player down the court. To improve your passing skills, practice the court player passing drills and those drills specifically designed for goalies.

GOALKEEPING SUCCESS STOPPERS

The most common technical errors you will make as a beginning goalie are listed here along with suggestions for correcting them. However, remember that the position equally demands the intangible qualities of confidence, composure, leadership, and courage.

ERROR	CORRECTION
Positioning in the Goal	
1. You bend at the waist, similar to a basketball defensive stance, with your hands low.	1. Stand tall with weight on the balls of your feet and shoulder-width apart. Hands are between shoulder and waist level.
2. You stand in the center of the goal line and do not move.	2. Follow the ball and move with quick shuffle steps in an arc between the goalposts.
Blocking High, Low, and Medium High Shots	
1. You feel off balance as the shot is taken.	1. When a player is ready to deliver the shot, stop moving and get in basic stance.
2. When attempting to catch a shot, it goes through your hands into the goal.	2. Stand in the basic goalie stance. Concentrate on making the block, not catching, then gain control of the ball quickly.
3. You lean, then reach rather than moving your body toward the ball.	3. Push off the leg farther from the ball.
4. You repeatedly contact the ball with your arm but it rebounds into the goal.	4. Stand one step from the goal line in basic position. As you move your arm(s) into the path of the ball, remember to go forward against the shot. Think, "Attack the ball."
5. You fail to use both your arm and leg to cover low shots.	5. Remember to shoot your leg in the path of the ball and cover with your arm and hand.
Blocking Wing Shots	
1. The ball goes between you and the goalpost.	1. From the wing the short corner is the easiest place to score. To prevent this easy goal, stand next to the goalpost, a ball's width away.
2. You don't use both your arm and leg to cover low shots.	2. Shoot your leg in the path of the ball and cover with your arm and hand.

GOALKEEPING

DRILLS

1. Partner Soccer

This drill works on turning your foot out to stop low shots. Face a partner 3 meters apart. Pass the ball back and forth with your feet, as a soccer player would pass a soccer ball. Concentrate on controlling the ball using the inside of your foot.

Success Goal = 30 seconds in control of ball ___

Success Check
• Move to the ball ___
• Contact ball with inside of your foot ___

To Increase Difficulty
• Increase the time for control by increments of 10 seconds.
• To increase the pace, decrease distance between partners.
• Play soccer tennis. Place a bench between you and your teammate and determine boundaries. Keep score as you do in tennis.

To Decrease Difficulty
• To slow the pace, increase the distance between partners.

2. Goalie Beginning Training Progression

This progression lets you concentrate on learning beginning goalie technique without the worry of being injured by a hard thrown shot. To keep the drill safe and to help you develop your confidence, ask your partner to control the speed and direction of the ball. Start by having your partner throw the ball gently, then gradually increase the speed as your confidence and technique improve. Have your partner wait for you to return to the basic goalie position before throwing the next ball. Stand about 3 meters apart.

a. Partner throws a ball at half speed at your face. Block the ball with both hands. Do not catch the ball.

b. Partner throws five balls to your high right and five to your high left. Block ball with both hands.

c. Partner rolls five balls to your right, then five to your left. Block the ball by turning your foot out and covering with your hand.

d. Partner rolls ball between your legs. Stand upright, block ball by jumping slightly forward and at the same time, bringing your feet together. Ball is blocked by hitting the front of your ankles.

e. Partner throws a low bouncing shot to the right and to the left. Block the ball by using the shoot and cover technique.

f. Partner throws the ball anywhere in the goal. Choose the correct technique to block the ball.

Success Goal = 10 balls blocked for each progression ____

✔ **Success Check**
• Stand tall ____
• Return to basic position after each attempt ____

To Increase Difficulty
• Have your partner start with 10 balls. Increase the speed of the shots and decrease the time between shots.
• Alternate throwing to the right and the left and high and low.

To Decrease Difficulty
• To increase safety and gradually build confidence, start by using a foam ball.

3. Line Shooting

This drill gives you repetitive practice at blocking high and low shots. By moving from one side to the other, this drill also helps you develop a feel for the size of the goal opening. Six shooters stand in one line in front of the goal. Each player has a ball and shoots one after the other, alternating shots right high and left high. The next time through, shoot right low and left low. Let the goalie recover to basic stance before shooting the next shot.

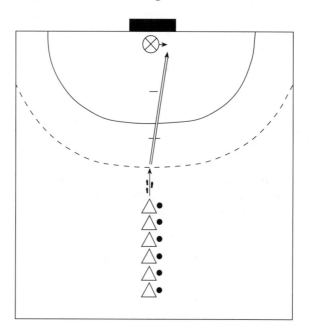

Success Goal = 4 out of 6 shots blocked ____

✔ **Success Check**
• Push off opposite leg ____
• Shoot and cover on low shots ____
• Recover quickly to basic position ____

To Increase Difficulty
• Players alternate right high, left low, then left high, right low.
• Similar to a fast-break, players dribble in and shoot a jump shot from the 6-meter line. Players should decrease the force of the shot by 50 percent and concentrate on placement in the goal.

To Decrease Difficulty
• Players decrease the speed of their shots.

4. 9-meter Set Shot Drill

This drill helps you work on positioning in the goal. It provides many consecutive repetitions for you to react to the ball and determine the proper technique to use. Six players, each with a ball, stand along the 9-meter line. Players shoot set shots in succession from left wing to right wing. Wait until the goalie recovers to basic stance before attempting the next shot. Move with quick shuffle steps from shooter to shooter and attempt to block each shot. Your movement should be in an arc from goalpost to goalpost as the ball moves from wing to wing. Repeat the drill starting from opposite side.

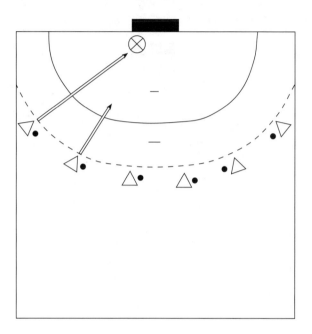

 **Success Goal** = 8 out of 12 shots blocked ____

Success Check
• Short quick shuffle steps ____
• Move in an arc between goalposts ____
• Recover to basic stance after each shot ____

To Increase Difficulty
• Add a defender in front of each shooter at the 6-meter line.
• Shooters move in and shoot from the 6-meter line.

To Decrease Difficulty
• Shooters decrease the speed and pace of their shots.

5. Wing Shooting

This drill works on positioning in the goal, especially in relation to the goalposts, and goalie technique for wing shots. Because of the limited angle and close proximity of the shooter, beginning wing shooters often lack accuracy, thus increasing the potential for injury to the goalie. Limit this drill to players who have developed their wing shooting accuracy with prior shooting practice without a goalie (see page 57). Two players with a ball stand in each wing, starting where the sideline meets the 9-meter line. The players shoot alternately from the right and left wing, forcing you to move quickly from one goalpost to the other. Shooters should wait for you to be in position before they shoot. Remember that it's important to protect the short corners and force the shooter to shoot for the more difficult long corners.

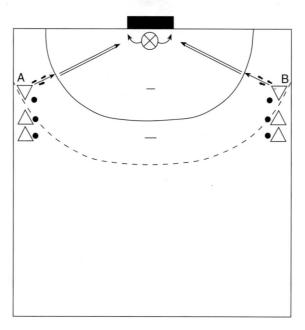

Blocking shots from the left and right wings

 **Success Goal** = 6 out of 10 blocked shots ____

 Success Check
• Move quickly, find goalpost ____
• Use forearm to protect your face ____
• Put weight on foot next to goalpost ____

To Increase Difficulty
• Add a wing defender against the shooters.
• Add a circle runner to shoot from the 6-meter line.

To Decrease Difficulty
• Shoot from only one side at a time.
• Shoot only bounce shots.
• Before each shot, designate the corner of the goal at which the wing will shoot.

6. Block, Pass, Defend Drill

This drill allows the goalie to work on initiating the fast-break after attempting to block a shot. Court players work on receiving a pass on the run with a defender close by and finishing the attack with a goal at the other end of the court. Three players stand without a ball in one wing, the other three stand in a row facing the goal in the CB position. The coach has some balls and stands to the side of the shooters. The first shooter attacks the goal and shoots from the 9-meter line. The goalie tries to block it. At the same moment the shot is taken, the first player in the wing starts running down the court. The goalie must forget about the ball that has just been shot, receive a new ball from the coach, and pass it out to the running player. The shooter must turn and run after the wing in an attempt to defend him or her. The two players return on the outside of the court and go to the opposite line (wing to shooter, shooter to wing). If a second goalie is available, end the drill with a shot on goal at the other end of the court.

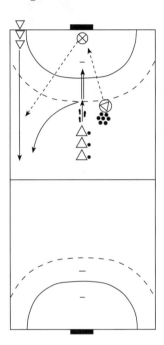

 **Success Goal** =

5 out of 10 blocked shots ____
8 out of 10 passes thrown with accuracy ____

✔ **Success Check**

• Concentrate on blocking the ball first ____
• Lead pass to the running player ____

To Decrease Difficulty

• Players shoot at half speed.

GOALKEEPING SUCCESS SUMMARY

Your play as the goalie greatly affects the psychological state of your teammates, and your overall performance considerably impacts your team's success. As your team's last line of defense, you must be able to block high, low, and medium high shots from all shooting positions and initiate the fast-break. Regardless of your success or failure, you must be a leader and display the intangible qualities of confidence, composure, and courage. Ask your coach or trained partner to rate your goalie technique according to the checklist items with the Keys to Success Figures 6.1 through 6.5.

INDIVIDUAL TACTICS: ATTACK AND DEFEND

O ne time down the floor, his defender sags and Magic pulls up to hit a 3-pointer. The next time, he penetrates the defense and dishes to Jabbar for a dunk. Another time, he makes a steal, leads the fast-break, and makes a beautiful behind the back pass to Byron Scott for a layup. Magic Johnson had great individual skills, but what set him apart, and helped make the Lakers great, was his ability to make good decisions about the execution of his skills. Choosing the proper skill and course of action to use at a given time and for a given situation is called tactics.

Step 7 will help you develop a good understanding of basic individual attack and defense tactics. The primary individual attack tactic is attacking the gap. You will learn how to anticipate and read the defense, maintain ball possession, and fake to help you attack the gap. Individual defense tactics relate to *controlling your defensive space*, which includes seeing ball and opponent, stepping out to meet the attacker, recovering to the 6-meter line, and moving in relation to the ball.

Why Are Individual Tactics Important?

During a game you will be confronted with many options on both ends of the court. Your ability to make good decisions concerning these options is just as important as proper execution of skills. If you are unable to make good decisions about when and where to perform your individual skills, you probably will not be successful, and your team will suffer the consequences.

Individual Attack Tactics— Attacking the Gap

As an attacking player your primary objective is to score goals and assist your teammates in scoring goals. The essential individual tactic toward achieving this is *attacking the gap*. A gap is a space between two defenders (see Figure 7.1).

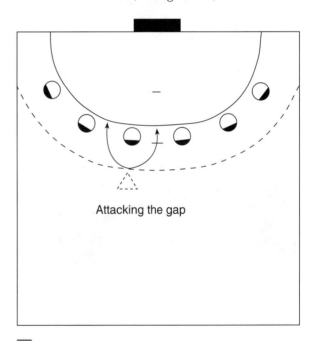

Attacking the gap

Figure 7.1 Attacking the gap.

Direct your actions at a gap for two reasons:

1. To try to break through the defense for a shot from the 6-meter line (see Figure 7.2).

Figure 7.2 Breaking between two defenders for a shot from the 6-meter line.

2. To draw the attention of two defenders, which creates a defensive imbalance and a numerical advantage for the offense. This means that if you are occupying the attention of two defenders, then one of your teammates must be unguarded for a scoring opportunity (see Figures 7.3a and b).

Use the following guidelines to assist you in recognizing and attacking the gap.

Anticipate

The best attack information is always gathered from the defense. Study the defense before receiving the ball so you can make quick decisions about the situation and take advantage of it. Anticipate so you can adjust your position according to the location and reaction of your defender and the location of the gap. As you receive the ball, you should know what course of action you want to take.

Maintain Ball Possession

Once in possession of the ball, maintaining a strong attacking position is vital. The most important consideration is that you be in a position that will protect the ball and enable you to make your next move as quickly and efficiently as possible. First rule is don't get too close to the defense and get tied up. The resulting free-throw disrupts the flow of your team's attack. Creating a workable space between you and your defender will help you protect the ball and give you time to make good decisions about your defender's actions. The shooting position naturally protects the ball because your body is between your defender and the ball (see Figure 7.4)

Figure 7.3a Occupying two defenders.

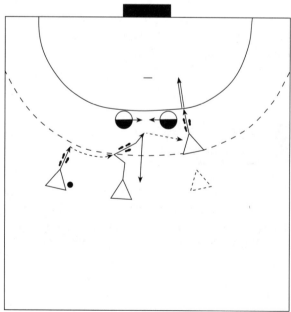

Figure 7.3b Draw two defenders and pass to open teammate.

Figure 7.4 Maintaining possession.

Fake

Sometimes, because of the good actions of your teammates, there is a big gap in front of you and all you have to do is receive a pass and go through. Other times you have to create your own gap. Faking is the chief means of getting your defender out of position to create more space in a gap. You can do this by changing the direction and pace of your movements.

How to Execute a Fake

Run to receive, catch the ball in midair, and land with both feet parallel to your shoulders for balance. When you land simultaneously on both feet after the catch, no steps are counted. This balanced position will allow you to change directions easily in an at-tempt to fake your defender. Let's say you want to fake your defender to the left and pass on the right. The footwork involved is important. Keep the ball in both hands at about waist level; step left transferring all your weight to your left foot and moving your shoulders and head in that direction also. As soon as your defender shifts in that direction, change directions quickly by pushing off your left foot to the right, and step past your defender with your right foot. Once past your defender, your third step will be toward the goal on your left foot, turning your shoulders perpendicular to the goal and raising the ball to shooting position. Once your defender is out of position you have to decide what to do next (see Figures 7.5a-e).

FIGURE 7.5 **KEYS TO SUCCESS**

FAKING

Preparation

1. Run to receive ___
2. Give teammate a target ___

a

b

3. Catch ball in midair ___
4. Land on both feet simultaneously ___

Execution

5. Step laterally on nonthrowing-hand foot ___

c

d

6. Step back in opposite direction past defender ___

7. Step toward goal on nonthrowing-hand foot ___

Follow-Through

e

8. Turn shoulders perpendicular to goal ___
9. Raise ball up and back ___
10. Decide to shoot or pass ___

Read the Defense

Once you've used a fake to get your defender out of position and you recognize the gap, you need to act quickly and decisively. The faster you can read the situation and act, the more likely you are to gain an advantage for yourself or a teammate. You must aggressively attack the gap with the intent to score. Being aggressive will allow you to either drive and shoot at the 6-meter line or draw the attention of the next defender, permitting a pass to an open teammate. Your mentality must be to "shoot first, pass second." Your decision to shoot, drive through the gap to the 6-meter line, or pass will depend on your court position relative to your defender and your teammates.

Attacking the Gap—Summary

Anticipate

1. Look at the location of the defenders.
2. Adjust your position.

Maintain Ball Possession

3. Create workable space—not *too* close.
4. Protect the ball.
5. Be a threat.

Fake

6. Change direction and pace.
7. Step past the defender toward goal.
8. Decide to pass or shoot.

Read the Defense

9. Move forward through the gap.
10. Think "shoot" first.
11. Pass if you draw two defenders.

Individual Defensive Tactics— Controlling Your Defensive Space

Generally, team handball defensive players shift as a unit as the strength of the attacking team moves. It's a zone defense, but within the zone each player has individual responsibility of controlling a certain space. Whenever an attacker comes into your "defensive space," that player then becomes your responsibility. Your defensive space reaches in all directions from your basic position, extending forward from the 6-meter line to the 9-meter line, and laterally to the defenders on either side of you (see Figure 7.6). Inability to control your defensive space will result in a breakdown of the entire defensive structure.

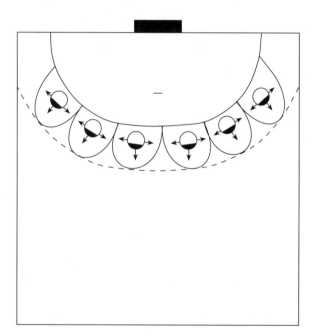

Figure 7.6 Individual defensive space.

Key tactical principles for controlling your defensive space are the following:

- *See ball and opponent.* Use your peripheral vision to be aware, at all times, of ball location and the opponent in your defensive space. Having this awareness will help you anticipate your opponent's actions, enabling you to defend in good position and timing.

- *Step out to meet an attacker with the ball* . As an attacker with the ball enters your space, aggressively step out to meet the attack. Quickly closing the space between you and your opponent gives less time for the attacker to make decisions and play the ball. Ideally, you should meet the attacker in the front of your space at the 9-meter line.

- *Stay between opponent and the goal* . To be an effective one-on-one defender, you must prevent your opponent from shooting or penetrating to the 6-meter line. You accomplish this by maintaining strong position between your opponent and the goal. The keys are proper checking and moving your feet.

- *Recover to 6-meter line* . When your opponent passes the ball to a teammate, you should then recover to the 6-meter line by shifting diagonally back in the direction of the pass. If you don't recover to the 6-meter line you leave a big open space close to the goal. Be aware of maintaining a good defensive stance throughout the movement.

- *Move in relation to the ball*. When your opponent doesn't have the ball, your basic defensive position is at the back of your defensive space along the 6-meter line. As the ball moves away from your defensive space, you will shift along the 6-meter line by shuffling in the direction the ball is moving. Move with short, quick shuffle steps, never crossing your feet and keeping them in contact with the floor.

Following is a summary of the key tactical principles for controlling your defensive space:

When Opponent Is Without the Ball

1. Shift along 6-meter line in direction of ball.
2. See the ball *and* your opponent.
3. Maintain good defensive stance.

When Opponent Has the Ball

1. Step out to meet the attacker near 9-meter line.
2. Recover diagonally to 6-meter line.

INDIVIDUAL TACTICS SUCCESS STOPPERS

The main focus of individual tactics is on decision making. Common errors that occur with individual attack and defense tactics are listed here along with suggestions for correction.

ERROR	CORRECTION
Individual Attack Tactics	
1. You attack the player directly in front of you.	1. Attack the gap. Go through to score or draw two defenders and pass.
2. You frequently interrupt the team attack by being fouled, which results in a free-throw call.	2. Don't get too close to the defense. Create a workable space. Protect the ball.
3. You take more than three steps when using a fake.	3. Run to receive, catch the ball in midair, and land simultaneously on both feet. No steps are counted when your feet hit the floor and you catch the ball in midair. You will have three steps to fake and attack.
4. You attack toward the gap but fail to look at the goalie.	4. You must attack with the intent to score. Keep the goalie in your vision and think shooting first. Move forward toward the gap, read the defense, then make a decision quickly to shoot, drive through, or pass.
Individual Defense Tactics	
1. You fail to step out to meet attacker with the ball at 9 meters.	1. Anticipate when your opponent will enter your defensive space. Aggressively step out to check an opponent with the ball.
2. You step out to 9 meters but fail to recover to the 6-meter line after the ball is passed.	2. After your opponent passes the ball, recover diagonally in the direction of the pass. This action supports the defender next to you and protects against shots from the 6-meter line.
3. A large space occurs between you and the teammate next to you on the 6-meter line.	3. Shift along the 6-meter line in the direction of the ball. Move with short, quick shuffle steps.

INDIVIDUAL TACTICS

DRILLS

1. Ten Passes Game

The purpose of this drill is to help you get comfortable with faking so it becomes second nature to you. The attackers use fakes without the ball to free themselves to receive a pass and fakes with the ball to free themselves to pass to a teammate. Play on the half-court using the 6-meter line as one boundary. If you are not on a court, mark a playing area 15 meters by 20 meters. Select two equal teams and match up player to player. Have your coach serve as referee and flip a coin to determine the first ball possession. The attacking team tries to complete 10 consecutive passes against the defense. If the ball is dropped, thrown out of bounds, or intercepted the other team takes possession. Turnovers also result from a 3-second rule violation and on the third free-throw due to defensive tie-ups. If the attacking team completes 10 passes it is awarded 1 point and keeps possession.

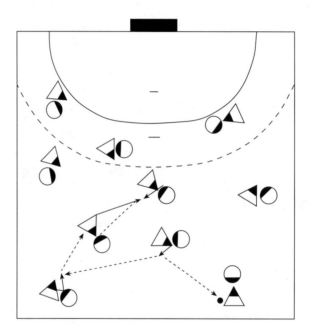

**Success Goal** = First team to 5 points wins ___

Success Check
• Be quick and deceptive ___
• Use shoulders, head, and feet to fake ___

To Increase Difficulty
• First team to 10 points wins.

To Decrease Difficulty
• Decrease the number of players on each team.

2. Fake and Drive

This drill will give you practice in creating workable space and in quickly changing your lateral faking movement into forward movement. The purpose is to help you be able to penetrate the gap and drive to the 6-meter line. Select a partner to participate with you in this drill. You stand in the center backcourt at about 12 meters with a ball and your partner on defense at about 6 meters. Place a cone about 2 meters on both sides of your partner to indicate the next defender and to show the gap. Pass the ball to your partner and, when your partner receives it, run to receive a return pass (see Figure a). After passing, your partner steps out to about 8 meters to meet your attack. From that point the defender should only react to the fake and allow you to step by on the drive. This is done to help you get a clear idea of when to change movement from the lateral fake to forward drive. When you're preparing to receive the return pass, think of creating a workable space—not too close or too far away from your defender. Time your attack so you receive the ball around 9 meters, then fake, drive to the 6-meter line, jump into the area, and shoot (see Figure b). At some point, you may need to dribble to gain three more steps to continue your drive. If your movement carries you directly to or outside the cone, it is an unsuccessful attempt.

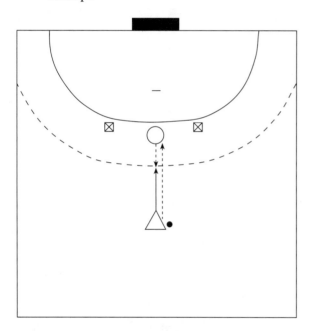

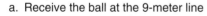

a. Receive the ball at the 9-meter line

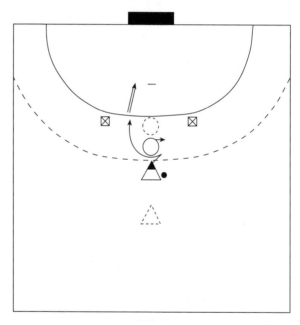

b. Fake, drive, and shoot

Success Goal =

5 attempts to fake left, drive right ____
5 attempts to fake right, drive left ____

Success Check

• Timing ____
• Create workable space ____
• Quick change lateral to forward movement ____

To Increase Difficulty

• Move the cones in 1 meter to narrow the gap.
• Play one-on-one, defense 100 percent. The player with the most successful fake and drives out of 10 is the winner.

To Decrease Difficulty

• Perform the drill at half speed.

3. Attack the Gap—Pass or Shoot

The purpose of this drill is to help you learn to read the defense and make good decisions accordingly. You and two teammates form an attacking team. Position one teammate in the left backcourt, one in the right backcourt, and you start in the center backcourt with a ball. Place three defenders on the 6-meter line, one defending each backcourt position. Place a cone 1 meter to the outside of the left backcourt and right backcourt defenders to indicate the next defenders. To begin, pass the ball to your defender, run to receive a return pass, fake right or left, and try to drive through the gap. For the purpose of the drill, the center backcourt defender should go with the fake and allow you into the gap. Now you must key on the next defender. If the defender does not move to close the gap, continue to drive to the 6-meter line and shoot (see Figure a). If the defender moves to close the gap, quickly pass to the attacking backcourt player who drives through the gap created by the displaced defender and shoots from the 6-meter line (see Figure b). Movement should not go past the cone. The backcourts switch positions after eight attacks, rotating from left to right. The defenders should do likewise. When all attackers have been in the center backcourt, switch offense and defense.

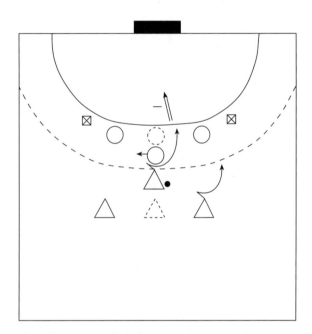

a. Center backcourt fakes and attacks the gap

b. Pass to right backcourt who shoots from the 6-meter line

Success Goal = 6 of 8 correct decisions ____

Success Check
• Key on the next defender ____
• Decide quickly ____

To Increase Difficulty
• Center backcourt defender plays 100 percent defense.
• Play a 3 vs. 3 scrimmage with no shooting from the backcourt. Direct all action toward penetrating a gap and driving to the goal area for a shot. Each team takes five possessions. Count 1 point per goal. The team with the most points wins.

4. Defense 6 meters-9 meters

This drill will help you get the feel for stepping out to check a shooter, as well as for the space between the 6-meter and 9-meter lines. If you are on a handball court, use the 6-meter and 9-meter lines. Otherwise, mark two lines 3 meters apart and 10 meters long. Shooters, up to six, stand along the 9-meter line, each with a ball. The first defender stands at the 6-meter line directly across from the first shooter. All other defenders line up behind the first. When shooter 1 raises the ball to shooting position, defender 1 steps out and checks the shooter. After making proper contact, retreat diagonally to the 6-meter line in front of shooter 2. Shooter 2 raises the ball to shooting position and defender 1 steps out, checks, retreats. Continue in this manner through the last shooter. As defender 1 gets in front of shooter 2, defender 2 steps out to shooter 1 and continues through the last shooter. When all defenders have gone through from left to right, defender 1 begins the next cycle from right to left. When you have completed five cycles, switch shooters and defenders.

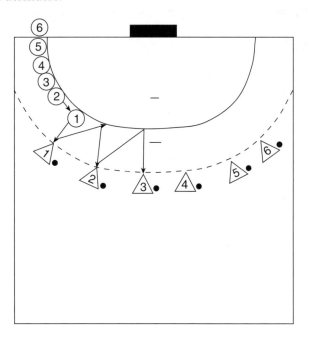

Step out to check a shooter

 **Success Goal** = 5 continuous cycles ___

Success Check
• Step out, make contact at 9-meter line ___
• Recover diagonally back to 6-meter line ___

To Increase Difficulty
• Increase the number of cycles.
• Shooter tries to fake and drive to the goal after defender makes contact.

To Decrease Difficulty
• Decrease the number of cycles.
• Do the drill with a partner. Step out, check your partner, and retreat directly to the 6-meter line. Do five times and switch shooter and defender.

5. Stepping Out and Recovering Basic Position

The purpose of this drill is to help you become familiar with the parameters of your defensive space and to work on the timing of stepping out to meet the attack as the ball arrives. You and a partner position yourselves in middle defense on the 6-meter line about 2 meters apart. Two other teammates stand directly in front of the two of you on the 9-meter line as passers (A and B). Two more passers (C and D) stand 2 meters to either side of them. Place a marker directly in front of the outside passers to indicate their defenders. When passer A slaps the ball and gets in shooting position, Defender #1 steps out to check. After the check, A passes to C or B, and Defender #1 recovers to the 6-meter line (see Figure a). If A passes to B, then Defender #2 steps out to check. B then passes to D or A, and Defender #1 and Defender #2 respond accordingly (see Figure b). When C has the ball, then Defender #2 should slide a little in that direction along the 6-meter line to close the gap. When D has the ball Defender #1 should do the same. All passers get in shooting position when in possession of the ball. Defender #1 and Defender #2 attempt to cover their defensive space as the passers continuously move the ball.

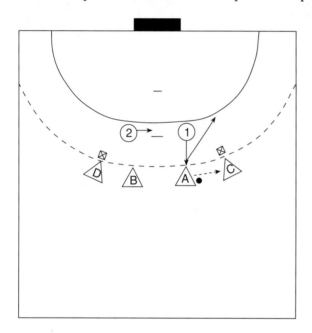

a. Defender #1 steps out and recovers to 6-meter line

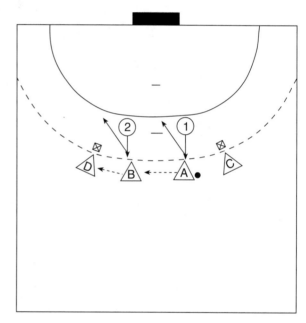

b. Defender #2 steps out, Defender #1 recovers to 6-meter line

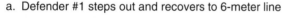
Success Goal = 30 seconds correctly covering defensive space ____

✔ Success Check
- Timing: meet the attacker as the ball arrives ____
- Recover diagonally to the 6-meter line ____

To Increase Difficulty
- C and D have the liberty to drive to the inside of their defense markers. D1 and D2 must step up to stop the drive.
- A and B have the liberty to shoot a set shot if their defender is late in stepping out.
- Do both of the above.

INDIVIDUAL TACTICS SUCCESS SUMMARY

Team handball is a game in which the success of the whole is highly dependent on how well each part works. Learning to use your individual skills in a tactical way is critical to team success. In attack this means not only creating scoring opportunities for yourself, but also assisting your teammates in scoring goals. Attack the gap aggressively and make good decisions regarding your options. Defensively, your primary concern is controlling your defensive space. Always be aware of the location of the ball and your opponent. Step out to meet the attacker with the ball, and recover in the direction of the ball to basic position to protect the 6-meter line. Ask your coach or trained partner to rate your technique according to the checklist items with the Keys to Success (see Figure 7.5). Also, ask your coach to evaluate your decision making in choosing correct skills and courses of action.

STEP 8

OFFENSIVE COMBINATIONS: SUPPORTING YOUR TEAMMATES

U p to this point, all the skills and tactics you've learned have been designed to develop your individual play. Individual skills and tactics are important, but rarely isolated. As the name implies, team handball is ultimately a team game requiring teamwork. To help your team score consistently, you must learn to use your individual attack skills and tactics in support of and in combination with your teammates.

Creating an "overload" is the principle that should guide all attack actions. Overload means that your team works to create a situation where attackers outnumber defenders in a given space. Ideally, this involves a player with the ball and a player in support against one defender. When an overload is created, everyone involved should move quickly and intelligently to exploit the situation. You can achieve an overload by executing three combinations: (1) supporting the player attacking the gap, (2) crossing, and (3) pick and roll.

Why Are Offensive Combinations Important?

Even though team handball is played 6 vs. 6, scoring opportunities usually involve small groups creating an overload situation. If played correctly, this numerical advantage should leave one player unguarded for an open shot. Practicing combinations in 4 vs. 3 and 3 vs. 2 situations will enhance your awareness of numerical advantages and your decision-making abilities about them. You will learn to recognize when you are open to shoot and when you should pass the ball to a teammate who is in a better position to score. Working in these small group situations will also help you learn how to move without the ball to get into better positions to attack and provide support for an attacking teammate. Coordinated actions with your teammates, coupled with good decision making, lay the groundwork for successful team attack.

How to Support the Player Attacking the Gap

Attacking the gap is an essential individual attack tactic. Equally important is your ability to support a teammate who is attacking a gap. When a teammate next to you attacks a gap and draws your defender, a 2 vs. 1 situation is created. Your awareness of the developing situation and anticipation of your defender's actions will help you take advantage of the overload.

As you see your defender move to close the gap, quickly run to receive a pass and attack the defensive space vacated by your defender. Timing in this action is important for two reasons: (1) to create an open passing lane for your teammate, and (2) to get into the vacated space before your defender can recover. Moving too early will put you too far in front of your teammate, allowing the defense to obstruct the passing lane. Moving too late will allow your defender to recover to his or her defensive space and even the numbers back to one-on-one.

If you receive the ball in proper timing to attack the vacated space and the next defender does not cover, you will have a clear path to penetrate the gap and shoot (see Figure 8.1a). If the next defender does cover, continue the overload by passing to the next teammate supporting your attack (see Figure 8.1b).

FIGURE
8.1

KEYS TO SUCCESS

SUPPORT THE PLAYER ATTACKING THE GAP
Execution

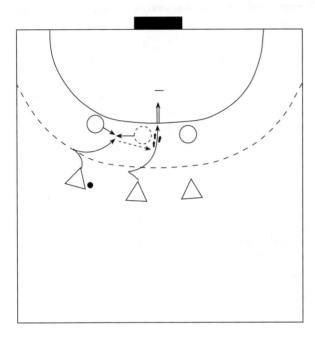

a

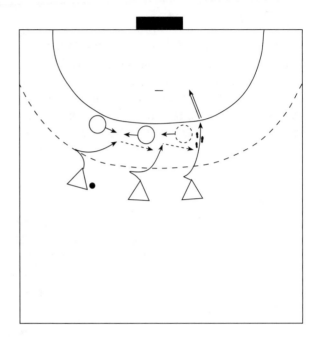

b

1. Anticipate your defender's actions ___
2. Run to receive ___
3. Next defender doesn't cover—penetrate and shoot ___

4. Next defender does cover—pass to the next supporting teammate ___

How to Execute Crossing

This strategy involves the crossing of two players, one over the path of the other, in an effort to confuse or slow down their defenders' actions. Generally, crossing takes place between two backcourt players, or a backcourt and a wing.

Let's say the center backcourt wants to cross with the left backcourt. With the ball, the center backcourt attacks toward the left backcourt's defender. The center backcourt must be a serious threat to score to hold his or her defender's attention and attract the left backcourt defender's attention as well. The left backcourt waits momentarily for the situation to develop, fakes toward the left wing to give the impres-

sion of continuing the attack, then runs to cross behind the center backcourt (see Figure 8.2). If the left backcourt shows this intention too early the defenders will recognize the situation and communicate the switch. The center backcourt waits until their paths intersect, then passes quickly to the left backcourt, who continues into the center backcourt's position looking to shoot. The confusion comes between the center backcourt's and left backcourt's defenders. If they don't communicate and switch responsibilities quickly enough, the left backcourt will be temporarily unguarded to shoot. The effectiveness of crossing depends on good timing and how well the two attackers read each other's actions.

FIGURE
8.2 | KEYS TO SUCCESS

CROSSING
Execution

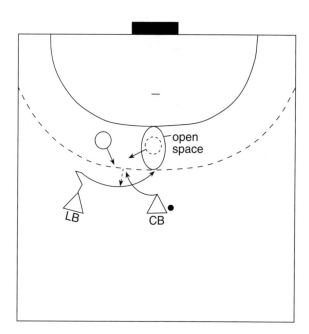

1. Attack toward left backcourt's defender ___
2. Left backcourt fakes toward left wing ___
3. Left backcourt runs behind center backcourt ___
4. Center backcourt passes to left backcourt as paths cross ___
5. Left backcourt looks for open shot ___

The Pick

Intelligent play of the circle runner is vital for any offense to be successful. The circle runner should constantly be looking to coordinate efforts with a backcourt player to free the backcourt for a scoring opportunity. The most effective technique for achieving this is the "pick." Using this tactic, the circle runner obstructs a backcourt defender's movement creating an opening for the backcourt to shoot.

How to Execute the Pick

In handball, set picks with your back to the defender so you can remain an offensive threat. In this position you are facing the action so you can follow the ball and keep your hands free to be a receiver. The key to setting a good pick is stability. Position your feet shoulder-width apart with your knees slightly bent to lower your center of gravity. This position will provide a stable base and help cushion your contact with the defender. Keep your hands up at chest level ready to receive a pass and slightly in front of your body for balance. Keep your torso upright with your head up and eyes on the ball (see Figure 8.3). You must be stationary when setting a pick. You may not use your hands, arms, legs, or hips to hold or push the defender.

FIGURE 8.3 · **KEYS TO SUCCESS**

THE PICK
Execution

1. Place your back to defender ___
2. Place feet shoulder width ___
3. Bend knees slightly, keep torso upright ___
4. Keep hands open at chest level ___
5. Head up, eyes on the ball ___

How to Execute the Pick and Roll

An important strategy involving the circle runner pick and the attack of a backcourt is the "pick and roll." When a defensive player steps out from the 6-meter line to check a backcourt, the circle runner pops out to set a pick on either side of the defender. It is important for the backcourt to set up the defender for the pick. As the backcourt attacks, fake the defender to the opposite side of where the pick will be set. This will momentarily move the defender away and give the circle runner more room to position. The backcourt then attacks back past the circle runner, thus moving the defender into the circle runner's pick. At this point the backcourt's defender is cut out of the action, leaving a 2 vs. 1 situation with the backcourt and circle runner against the next defender. If the next defender does not step out to meet the backcourt's attack, then the backcourt has a clear shot on goal (see Figure 8.4a). If the next defender does step out, the circle runner rolls into the open space created behind the two defenders who are out and receives a pass from the backcourt for a shot from the 6-meter line (see Figure 8.4b).

FIGURE 8.4

KEYS TO SUCCESS

THE PICK AND ROLL
Execution

1. Backcourt fakes defender ___
2. Circle runner pops out to pick ___
3. Backcourt attacks past the pick ___

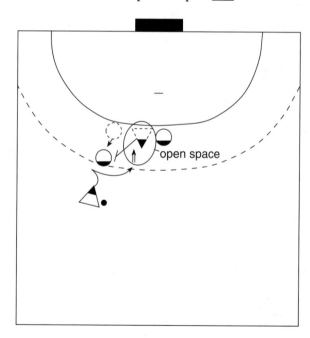

a

b

4. Next defender does not step out—backcourt shoots ___

5. Next defender does step out—circle runner rolls for pass and shot ___

OFFENSIVE COMBINATIONS SUCCESS STOPPERS

The most common errors in supporting the player attacking the gap, crossing, and doing pick and roll are listed here along with suggestions for correcting them.

ERROR	CORRECTION
Supporting the Player Attacking the Gap	
1. You start running to receive too early or you do not move at all.	1. Run to receive when your defender moves to close the gap on your attacking teammate. Moving early puts you too far in front of your teammate, allowing the defense to obstruct the passing lane. Not moving at all allows defense to easily recover and stop the attack.
Crossing	
1. As the crossing left backcourt, you fail to set up your defender by faking before crossing with the center backcourt.	1. Wait momentarily for the center backcourt to draw attention of your defender. Fake toward the left wing, then cross behind the center backcourt.
2. As the center backcourt, you pass too early to the left backcourt.	2. Wait until your path intersects with the left backcourt to pass the ball. Passing too early allows the defense to adjust to the crossing action.
Pick and Roll	
1. You set the pick facing the defender.	1. Set the pick with your back to the defender so you are facing the action and your hands are free to catch a pass.
2. As the backcourt, you fail to set up your defender with a fake.	2. Before the pick by the circle runner, fake your defender in the opposite direction to give the circle runner more room to position the pick.
3. As the circle runner, you are late getting out to set the pick.	3. As the defender steps out, you move out to set the pick.

OFFENSIVE COMBINATIONS

DRILLS

1. Overload Support: 4 vs. 3

The purpose of this drill is to practice attacking the gap and the timing of supporting teammates attacking the gap. Place two cones on the court as shown in the diagram to designate the playing area. You and three other players form an offensive team consisting of a left wing and three backcourt players. Three other players and a goalie form a team and play defense. Play 4 vs. 3 with regular handball rules. The one restriction is that the offense can only play by attacking the gap and supporting each other. No one can shoot from the backcourt. All scores must come by driving through a gap and shooting from the 6-meter line. Each shot attempt, defensive tie-up, or other turnover counts as one possession. Play five possessions then switch offense and defense. The wing and goalie should not switch but play offense and defense for both teams respectively.

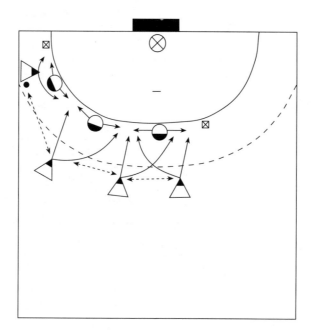

**Success Goal** = Score more points than the opposition ___

To Increase Difficulty
• Add a defender and play 4 vs. 4.

Success Check
• Attack the gaps ___
• Support your teammates ___

2. Crossing: 2 vs. 1

The purpose of this drill is to help you practice the timing and ball handling involved in crossing with a teammate. Place two cones on the court as shown in the diagram to designate the playing area. Select two teammates and a goalie to play with you. One teammate begins play on defense and the other plays center backcourt with you playing in the left backcourt. You start with the ball in the left backcourt and pass to the center backcourt, who attacks to the left. The defender steps out to meet the center backcourt's attack. In good timing with the center backcourt's attack, you cross behind, receive a pass, and shoot a set shot or jump shot through the opening. Perform the drill seven times, then rotate positions clockwise until each player has played all positions. The goalie remains in the goal through all rotations. You receive 1 point each time you and your teammate perform the skill flawlessly and an extra point for scoring a goal, with 14 points possible.

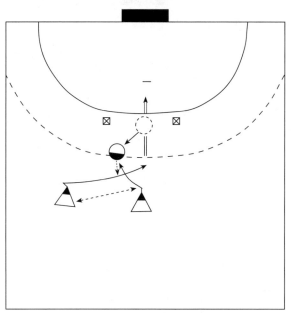

Success Goal = 10 of 14 possible points scored ___

Success Check
• Timing—cross when the defender steps out to meet your teammate's attack ___

To Increase Difficulty
• Play 2 vs. 1. The attackers must begin with crossing, but the defender may play the situation as she wishes. The attackers must decide who has the best scoring opportunity. For instance, if the defender doesn't step out, the center backcourt will be unguarded, so he or she should decide to keep the ball and continue attacking instead of passing. Attackers receive 1 point for a score, and the defender receives 2 points for stopping the attack. A missed shot has no point value but is counted as a possession. Play five possessions and rotate the same as in the original drill. Each player keeps track of all of his or her points throughout the rotation. The player with the most cumulative points is the winner.

To Decrease Difficulty
• Play without defense.

3. Attack the Gap and Crossing: 4 vs. 3

The purpose of this drill is to practice the combination of crossing in a gamelike situation. Place two cones on the court as shown in the diagram to designate the playing area. To begin, you and three other players form an attacking team consisting of a right wing and three backcourt players. Three other players and a goalie form a team and play defense. Play 4 vs. 3 with regular handball rules. The offense can only play by attacking the gap and supporting or executing crossing. The center backcourt may cross with either backcourt. A goal scored by crossing equals 2 points. A goal scored by driving through a gap equals 1 point. Play five possessions, then switch offense and defense. The wing and the goalie should not switch but play offense and defense for both teams, respectively.

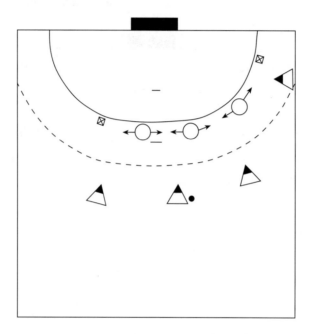

 **Success Goal** = Score more points than the opposition ___

 **Success Check**
• Execute crossing ___
• Make good decisions ___

 **To Increase Difficulty**
• Add a defender and play 4 vs. 4.

4. Circle Runner Pick Drill

The purpose of this drill is for the circle runner to practice the technique for setting a pick and for the backcourt and circle backcourt to practice the timing of the circle runner pick. You will need three teammates to participate with you in this drill. Place a passer in the center backcourt with a good supply of balls, a shooter in the left backcourt, and a circle runner in the middle on the 6-meter line. The other player is the defender and should be on the 6-meter line directly in front of the left backcourt. Place a cone on the 6-meter line left of the circle runner to designate the next defender. The left backcourt runs to receive a pass from the center backcourt, and the defender steps out to meet the attack. While the defender is moving out, the circle runner pops out to establish a position to set the pick. The left backcourt fakes left to draw the defender away from the circle runner, then steps right to run the defender into the pick. With the defender out of the action, the left backcourt shoots a jump shot. Repeat the drill seven times, then rotate clockwise, moving center backcourt to left backcourt, left backcourt to defender, defender to circle runner, and circle runner to center backcourt.

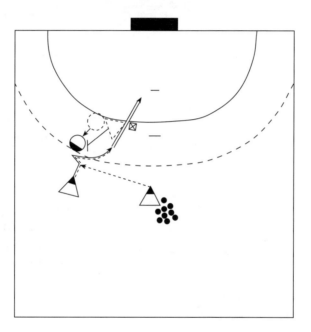

Success Goal = 5 out of 7 properly executed picks ___

Success Check
- Circle runner coordinates timing with backcourt attack ___
- Set pick with your back ___
- Hold hands chest high ___
- Place feet shoulder-width apart, bend knees ___

To Increase Difficulty
- Execute the pick and roll. When the left backcourt steps past the pick, the circle runner rolls toward the 6-meter line, receives a pass from the left backcourt, and shoots a fall shot from the 6-meter line.
- Play 3 vs. 2 working the pick and roll.

To Decrease Difficulty
- Put a cone at the 9-meter line to replace the defender.

5. All Combinations: 4 vs. 3

The purpose of this drill is to practice the execution of all combinations in a gamelike situation. Use the same set-up, rules, and scoring as in Drill 1. The offense tries to score using all combinations.

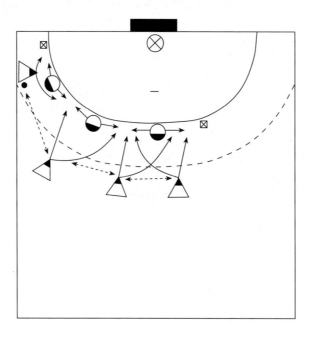

Success Goal = Score more points than the opposition ___

Success Check
• Create overload through the execution of attack the gap and support, crossing, and pick and roll ___
• Timing: support your teammates ___
• Make good decisions ___

To Increase Difficulty
• Replace the cone in the wing with a defender and play 4 vs. 4. Now the wings will play offense and defense for their respective teams.

OFFENSIVE COMBINATIONS SUCCESS SUMMARY

Creating an overload, working for a situation in which attackers outnumber defenders, is the principle that should guide all offensive actions. Players achieve this by using their individual skills and tactics in support of and in combination with each other. The small group combinations of pick and roll and crossing are two tactics you can employ to create an overload. If they are executed correctly, a 2 vs. 1 situation develops, freeing you or a teammate for a shot. Intelligently coordinated actions with your teammates lay the groundwork for successful team attack. Ask your coach or trained partner to rate your technique according to the checklist items with the Keys to Success (see Figures 8.1 through 8.4).

STEP 9

DEFENSIVE COMBINATIONS: HELP AND COMMUNICATION

Whether playing in attack or defense the focal point is always the ball, because only the ball can score. In attack this involves a small group of players working together to score goals and on defense a small group working to prevent goals. Effective defense requires the successful execution of three small group tactics: the defensive help triangle, taking over–passing on procedure, and switching.

Why Are Defensive Combinations Important?

When you step out and check the attacker in your defensive space, you create a hole behind you in the defensive structure—a vulnerable spot that the attackers could easily exploit. The defensive help triangle provides maximum defensive coverage at the point of the attack. The objective is to put pressure on the ball and fill any hole in the defense before an attacker can take advantage of it.

Just the presence of the circle runner is enough to disrupt defensive unity, but it is the circle runner's movement in attack that presents the toughest problems for defenders. Never leave the circle runner unguarded. The circle runner will move in and out of many defensive spaces trying to create openings in the defense structure.

To avoid confusion and to make sure one player is always responsible for the circle runner, all players must have command of the take over–pass on procedure.

Switching is the act of changing the opponent guarded. Anytime one attacker is moving into your defensive space and one is moving out simultaneously, or when two attackers are moving in the same space at the same time, the defenders responsible must switch opponents to avoid an overload.

How to Execute the Defensive Help Triangle

The help triangle is formed by one defender positioned on the ball at the point of the triangle and two defenders positioned behind that defender providing help on either side (see Figure 9.1). When a defender steps out, it is the responsibility of the teammates on either side to squeeze in slightly to fill the hole created on the 6-meter line. The "help" defenders serve as the "point" defender's safety valves. If the point defender is beaten, the help defenders are in position to step out and prevent a shot or a penetration to the goal area. Covering the hole also helps prevent other attackers from moving into the open space for a direct pass and high-percentage shot from the 6-meter line.

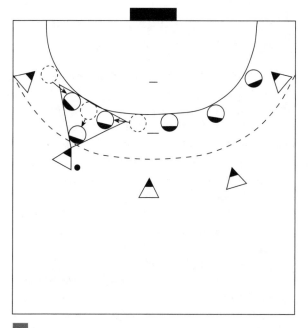

Figure 9.1 The defensive help triangle.

Communication in the Triangle

Communication is a key element in effectively executing the defensive help triangle. Communication is a two-way street. All three defenders should constantly talk to one another. Talking ensures that each knows who is stepping out and who is staying back to defend the 6-meter line. Executing the help triangle can be confusing at times, particularly when there are a circle runner and an attacking backcourt playing in the same defensive space. Figure 9.2a illustrates this situation.

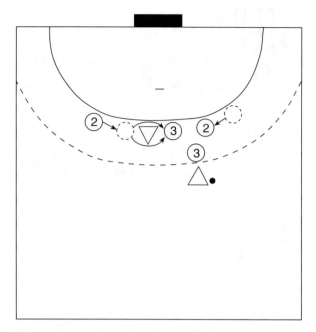

Figure 9.2b   Executing the help triangle.

How to Execute the Take Over–Pass On Procedure

When the circle runner moves into your defensive space, you must take over the physical control of this player from your teammate. Slide a little toward your teammate to receive the circle runner. There will be a brief moment when both you and your teammate guard the circle runner (see Figure 9.3a). To defend the circle runner, position your body between him or her and the goal. Use your torso and open hands to maintain contact, and always be ready to deflect a pass. This position is similar to playing post defense in basketball (see Figure 9.3b). Even though there is a lot of body-to-body contact, remember that you play good defense with your feet. Keep your feet moving to maintain position between the circle runner and the goal.

As the circle runner moves out of your space, verbally communicate the circle runner's movements to the next defender. Maintain physical contact until you can pass on the physical control of the circle runner to your teammate (see Figure 9.3c). If you execute this procedure effectively, you will maintain visual and physical contact with the circle runner at all times, creating fewer problems for the defense as a whole.

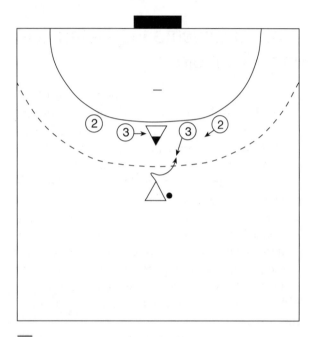

Figure 9.2a   Circle runner and backcourt in same defensive space.

The circle runner is between the number 3 defenders, and the center backcourt has the ball. The location of the circle runner and center backcourt presents a dilemma about coverage for the number 3 defenders. In this situation, two things have to happen to prevent a scoring opportunity: (1) you must put pressure on the ballhandler, and (2) you must control the circle runner. Anticipation and early communication are the keys. The number 3 defenders must decide who will step out to check the center backcourt and who will defend the circle runner. If you neglect either attacker he or she will have a clear scoring opportunity. To complete the help triangle, the number 2 defender on the side of the number 3 defender who stepped out should squeeze in to fill the hole on the 6-meter line (see Figure 9.2b).

FIGURE
9.3

KEYS TO SUCCESS

TAKE OVER–PASS ON PROCEDURE

Take Over

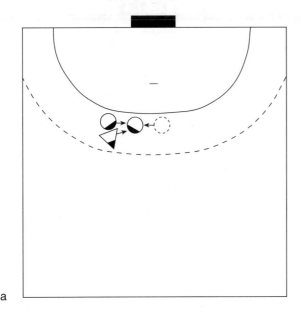

a

Guard

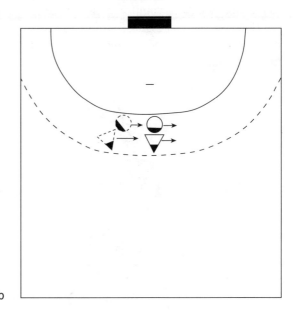

b

1. Communicate ___
2. Slide toward your teammate ___
3. Take over physical control ___

4. Position body between circle runner and goal ___
5. Body-to-body contact ___
6. Keep ball-side hand in the passing lane ___
7. Move your feet ___

Pass On

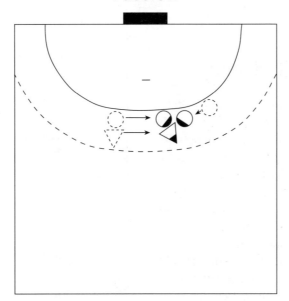

c

8. Communicate movement ___
9. Maintain contact ___
10. Pass on ___

If the circle runner receives a pass, your objective is to stop the threat of a shot. In this situation, you will need to immediately tie up the circle runner even though the result will be a free-throw. To prevent the circle runner from turning to shoot, maintain body-to-body contact with your torso, and try to get your hands on the ball (see Figure 9.4). This is a time when a slight infringement of the rules is better than giving up a shot from the 6-meter line.

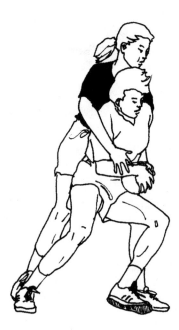

Figure 9.4 Tying up the circle runner.

How to Execute Switching

Common examples of situations that require switching are crossing and pick and roll (see Figures 9.5 and 9.6). Switching is not always easy, especially when attackers are moving quickly and executing flawlessly. There will be a moment during the switch when the attackers will be unguarded. It is important that this be as short a time as possible. To help with this, there are two points to remember when performing a switch. First, communicate to your teammate that you are going to switch. Verbally acknowledge all communication so each defender is certain of each other's attention to the situation.

Secondly, before assuming the responsibility of another player, you must stay with the player you're guarding until you are absolutely sure that the switch will be made.

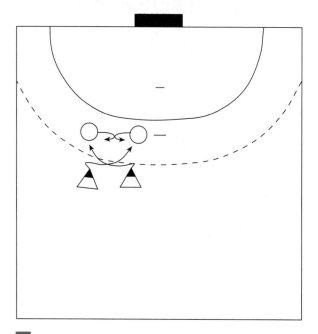

Figure 9.5 Defenders switching on a crossing action by the attackers.

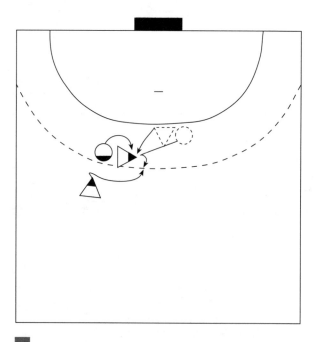

Figure 9.6 Defenders switching on a pick and roll.

OFFENSIVE COMBINATIONS SUCCESS STOPPERS

ERROR	CORRECTION
Defensive Help Triangle	
1. You leave the circle runner or backcourt unguarded in your defensive space.	1. You and your teammates must communicate your intended actions to cover attackers in your space.
2. The point defender is beaten one-on-one and BC scores from the 6-meter line.	2. Squeeze in behind the point defender to provide help.
Take Over and Pass On	
1. Circle runner is open on the 6-meter line for a pass and shot.	1. Communicate the circle runner's movements to teammates and maintain contact with the circle runner at all times.
Switching	
1. You fail to switch, resulting in an attacker being open to shoot.	1. Communicate the switch with your teammate and stay with your player until you are absolutely sure the switch will be made.

DEFENSIVE COMBINATIONS

DRILLS

1. Circle Runner Coverage: 3 vs. 2

The purpose of this drill is to practice coordinating efforts with a teammate to ensure coverage of the ballhandler and circle runner at all times. You and a partner form a team and position yourselves on defense at the 6-meter line. Position a circle runner in between the two of you. Two other teammates complete the attacking team by positioning themselves across from the defenders at the 9-meter line. The attackers continuously pass the ball between themselves while the defenders step out and recover so the ballhandler and circle runner are covered at all times. The passer should raise the ball to shooting position and allow the defender to check before passing. The goal for the defenders is to prevent a completed pass to the circle runner in a 30-second period. If this is achieved the defenders receive 1 point, and the teams switch roles for another 30-second period. If a pass is completed the drill immediately stops, the attacking team receives 1 point, and the teams switch roles. The circle runner does not switch and plays offense for both teams. Continue the drill until one team earns 5 points.

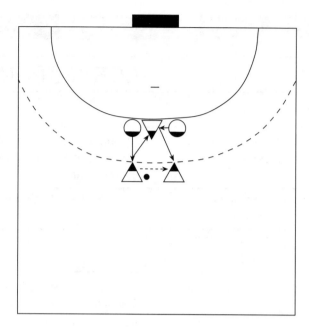

Step out, check backcourt,
recover to defend circle runner

Success Goal = The first team to earn 5 points wins ___

Success Check
• Communicate ___
• Step out and recover ___
• Keep contact with circle runner ___

To Increase Difficulty
• Extend drill time to 45 seconds.

2. Take Over and Pass On Drill

The purpose of this drill is to learn to take over control of the circle runner from a teammate, defend the circle runner through your defensive space, and pass on control of the circle runner to the next defender. You will need two teammates to play with you on defense. Designate each player's defensive space by placing four markers 3 meters apart just behind the 6-meter line. You begin in defensive space B on the 6-meter line, with your teammates filling the spaces on either side. A group of five attackers (circle runners) stands outside space A. Your coach stands with a ball at 10 meters to pass. The first circle runner steps into space A with his or her back to the goal and hands up ready to catch. Defender A stands between the attacker and the goal in good circle runner defense position. The circle runner slides to the right, and defender A moves with the circle runner through his or her space. As the circle runner approaches your space, slide over to take over the circle runner from defender A. Remember to communicate with each other. Defender A passes on the circle runner as you take over physical control by establishing circle runner defense position. The circle runner will be looking to receive a pass while moving through your defensive space. Your job is to maintain good position and prevent the circle runner from receiving a pass. If the circle runner receives a pass, immediately execute a tie-up, preventing a turn for a shot or a pass back out. Play should stop on a tie-up. Return the ball to the passer, and continue the game with the next circle runner. As the circle runner approaches space C, communicate with your teammate as he or she slides toward you to take over the circle runner. Continue in this manner until all five circle runners have gone through; then repeat, starting from the opposite side to complete the cycle. You are playing against the five circle runners collectively. You receive 1 point for a successful take over–pass on without a completed pass and 1 point for a successful tie-up if the circle runner receives a pass. The circle runners receive 2 points for a completed pass.

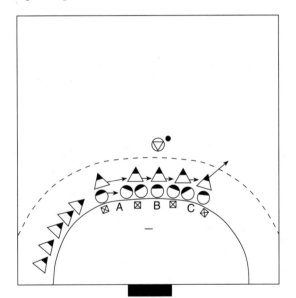

![Success Goal icon] **Success Goal** = Most points wins:

Your points ____

Circle runner points ____

To Decrease Difficulty

• Play without a passer.

![Success Check icon] **Success Check**

• Maintain body-to-body contact ____

• Keep good position, move your feet ____

• Communicate ____

3. Switching Drill

In this drill you learn how to execute a defensive switch with a teammate. You and a teammate position yourselves in the middle on defense at the 6-meter line. A group of attackers line up in each wing. One wing starts dribbling around the goal area between the 6-meter and 9-meter lines. The opposite wing begins running around the goal area at the same time. The dribbler passes to the other wing as their paths approach each other in the middle of the court. Take responsibility of the attacker in your defensive space, and switch when necessary. Communicate the switch to your teammate.

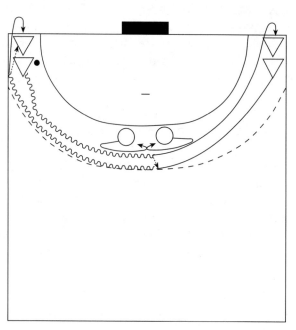

Making the moment during the switch when the
attackers are unguarded as short as possible

Success Goal = 10 correctly executed switches ___

✔**Success Check**
• Defend attacker in your space ___
• Communicate ___
• Switch responsibility of attackers ___

To Increase Difficulty
• Perform switch against pick and roll.
• Perform switch against backcourt crossing.

4. Defensive Triangle Drill: 4 vs. 5

This drill will help you learn to execute the help triangle. Place a marker, as shown in the figure, to designate the playing area. Position a circle runner on the 6-meter line to play offense for both teams. Three of your teammates form an attacking team and position themselves in the left wing, left backcourt, center backcourt, and right backcourt positions. You and three teammates form another team and position yourselves on defense at the 6-meter line. Get a goalie to tend goal for both teams. The attackers move the ball using the piston movement looking to shoot, or pass the ball to the circle runner. The defenders execute the help triangle each time the ball is passed. The objective for the defense is to prevent any shots from the backcourt and prevent any completed passes to the circle runner in a 30-second period. If they achieve this, they receive 1 point and the teams switch roles. If the attackers score a goal from the backcourt or complete a pass to the circle runner they receive 1 point and the teams switch roles.

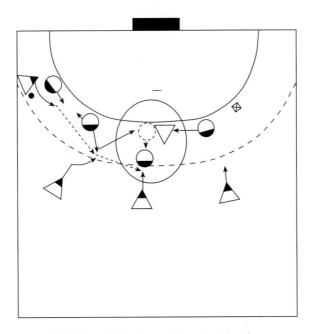

Players shift to form defensive triangle

 **Success Goal** = First team to 10 points wins ___

Success Check
• Communicate all actions ___
• Help the defenders squeeze in ___
• Cover the circle runner ___

To Increase Difficulty
• Increase drill time to 45 seconds.

To Decrease Difficulty
• Remove the circle runner and play 4 vs. 4.

DEFENSIVE COMBINATIONS SUCCESS SUMMARY

The purpose of defense is to prevent goals, so the focus of your team's efforts must be the ball and all the potential scorers in the immediate vicinity. Small group defense tactics are designed to ensure that this coverage occurs. Properly executing the defensive help triangle (see Figure 9.1), take over and pass on procedure (see Keys to Success items in Figure 9.3), and switching (see Figures 9.5 and 9.6) allows you to aggressively defend a ballhandler in your defensive space with the peace of mind of knowing you've got help. Communication is the key to ensuring that all activity is covered. Verbally let your teammates know if you are stepping out, switching, or taking over and passing on and expect the same from them. Remember that communication is a two-way street, so it's equally important that all communication be verbally acknowledged. Letting your teammates know that you hear them and understand their intentions allows them to confidently carry out their actions.

STEP 10

TRANSITIONS: FAST-BREAK AND QUICK RETREAT

Transition is the period of moving from one activity or place to another.

Team handball is a fast-paced game, so there are numerous transitions that occur during the course of a contest. The fast-break is a transition from defense to attack, and the quick retreat is a transition from attack to defense. Anatoli Yevtushenko, coach of the 1988 Soviet Union Olympic champions and longest-serving team handball coach in the world, says, "Our aim is to score as many goals as possible in fast-break so that we don't have to play against an active, aggressive, organized defense." This statement strongly emphasizes that your team's ability to make quick and intelligent transitions to attack and defense can mean the difference between winning and losing. Step 10 addresses the primary and secondary fast-breaks and the three stages of quick retreat.

Why Are Transitions Important?

The successful completion of a fast-break means more than just quickly upping the score. A defensive team suddenly becoming a successful attacking team has definite psychological consequences. Scoring on the fast-break stimulates and motivates your team, while the opposition becomes demoralized and discouraged. Constant fast-breaking forces the opposition to adjust its attack strategy, perhaps becoming more cautious. Also, constantly defending against the fast-break can physically wear a team down. Mastering the primary and secondary fast-break will add a dynamic dimension to your attack.

The cumulative effect of your team's inability to master quick retreat and consistently stop the fast-break can be discouraging. The negative psychological consequences can be potentially damaging to team performance on both ends of the court. For any team, transition to defense is a vulnerable time. When your team loses ball possession, you know the opposition is going to try to fast-break. If your team doesn't react immediately and intelligently to this pressure, the opposition will be able to pick up some easy goals. Any team will give up a fast-break goal from time to time, but working hard on quick retreat will prevent easy scores from a fast-break.

The Fast-Break

When the defense gains possession of the ball because of a blocked shot, interception, or rule violation, the team is at that moment in a position to begin a fast-break. The team handball fast-break involves the same characteristics as those in basketball, using speed and as few passes as possible to outmaneuver the defense down the court for a quick score. This can be accomplished by executing either the primary or secondary fast-break. The primary fast-break is achieved when one player breaking away from the defense receives a pass from the goalie or other teammate and attacks the goal alone. The secondary fast-break is more of a team effort—all players move up the court quickly in an effort to obtain an easy scoring opportunity against the retreating defense. To be an effective fast-breaking team requires superb physical conditioning, mental discipline, and much practice. If your team is committed to making the fast-break a consistent part of your game, the payoff will be well worth the effort.

How to Execute the Primary Fast-Break

The goalie plays a major role in transition from defense to attack, because most fast-break opportunities occur after a goalie save. A good fast-break depends on the goalie's ability to quickly recover a blocked shot, make the choice of a receiver, and accurately pass the ball to a breaking player. The wings are usually the faster players and take the lead on the fast-break. As soon as the shot is taken, unless either is directly involved in defending the shooter, the wings quickly break from their positions and sprint directly down the court. The wings should not break their paths toward the middle of the court until they reach the midcourt area. Maintaining this width makes the defenders' jobs more difficult. The goalie's first look should be to a wing, but only make the pass if the player is wide open. Upon receiving the pass, the wing should accelerate, by the most direct route available, toward the center of the goal. Because the wing is often alone in this situation, advancing the ball may require dribbling. To finish the fast-break, jump into the goal area and score (see Figure 10.1)

How to Execute the Secondary Fast-Break

If the goalie is unable to make a direct pass to a breaking wing, he or she should throw an outlet pass to one of the remaining players. These remaining four players constitute the secondary break. When the ball is shot, the backcourts and circle runner should hesitate and maintain their defensive positions to protect against rebounds. When possession of the ball is secured, they break down court as a second wave. When the goalie completes the outlet pass, the second wave should pass the ball quickly up the court in an attempt to score before the opposition can fully recover and organize their half-court defense.

Spacing and depth are two important components involved in successfully executing the secondary fast-break. Players should space themselves so there is enough distance between two teammates to prevent one defender from easily defending both. When moving the ball up the court, the fastest way is in a straight line, and you should take that route if possible (see Figure 10.2).

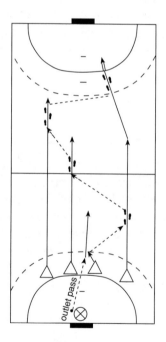

Figure 10.2 The secondary fast-break.

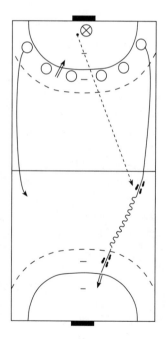

Figure 10.1 The primary fast-break.

Oftentimes, however, in the secondary break you have to face retreating defenders along the way, who you must avoid if the break is to continue. This requires use of a more tactical approach to confuse defenders and slow them down. A way to accomplish this is by well-coordinated changes of position with your teammates (see Figure 10.3).

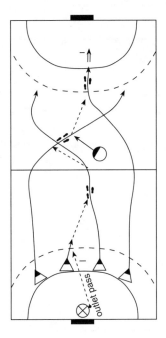

Figure 10.3 A tactical solution for avoiding a defender during the secondary fast-break.

To provide depth, players should stagger themselves as they move up the court. Depth is important for two reasons: (1) if the lead players' attack is being stifled, the trailing players can analyze the situation and adjust without slowing down, keeping pressure on the unorganized defense, and (2) to ensure that there will be at least one player back to defend in case a turnover occurs. If the primary and secondary fast-breaks do not create a clear scoring opportunity, players should assume their positions and organize the attack.

How to Execute Quick Retreat

When your team loses possession of the ball, the mentality must immediately shift to defense. No sulking about a missed shot or turnover; every player must react quickly. Three stages characterize making the quick retreat and defending the fast-break.

First, pressure the player with the ball. This will temporarily disrupt the fast-break, giving all other defenders a chance to establish good defensive positions. Only the player closest to the ballhandler should attempt this defensive pressure. Often the ballhandler will be the goalie who is inside the goal area. In this case, designate a player to mirror the goalie's movements, attempting to obstruct his or her vision. When the ballhandler passes the ball, the player applying pressure retreats quickly to the defensive end of the floor.

In the second stage of the transition, while initiation of the fast-break is being delayed, all other players should hustle back to the defensive end of the court. During this retreat, pay attention to defending the most immediate danger, so guarding an opponent along the way may be necessary. All players should keep an eye on the ball at all times and communicate with each other. Always make sure that the player with the ball is guarded, as well as other players in potentially dangerous positions. In the early stages of retreat, player-to-player defense is most practical. This is especially true in covering the breaking wings and preventing them from receiving a direct pass from the goalie (see Figure 10.4).

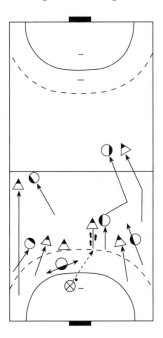

Figure 10.4 Quick retreat.

If an outlet pass is completed and the fast-break is in progress, the first players back must guard the leaders of the break and try to slow down the attack until teammates can recover and help. These players may be momentarily charged with defending the entire goal area, but pay particular attention to the most vulnerable area directly in front of the goal. They should try to force the ball toward the wing areas so the goalie will have a better chance for a save (see Figure 10.5).

The third phase involves organizing the zone. During quick retreat, especially if defending against a fast-break, players often find themselves out of their regular defensive positions. During this short time of disorganization, everyone must work together to provide normal defensive coverage. The first players back take positions along the 6-meter line establishing a "wall" in front of the goal, and from there do their best to keep pressure on the ball and protect danger zones until all teammates can get back. When all players are back to the 6-meter line, organization of the zone begins with each player shifting to his or her regular defensive position. Do the organizing quickly, but without jeopardizing defensive strength. Shifting occurs one position at a time by players who are not directly involved in defending the ball. *Communication is vital.* This re-organization can be overseen by the goalie who, by virtue of his or her position, can survey the situation and give instructions to teammates. If a lull in the attack occurs quickly, such as a free-throw, then all players should scramble to their normal defensive positions (see Figure 10.6).

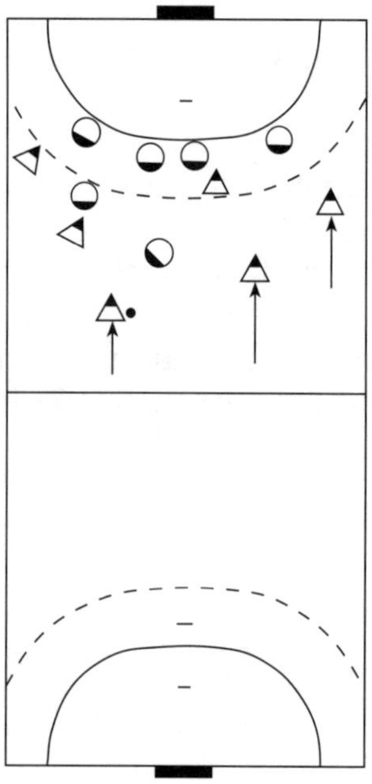

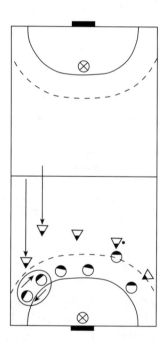

Figure 10.5 Concentrate defense in front of goal.

Figure 10.6 Players switch positions safely (ball on opposite side of court).

TRANSITION DRILLS

DRILLS

1. Over the Shoulder Pass and Catch

The purpose of this drill is to help you learn to catch the ball over your shoulder while running straight ahead, and to help you learn to pass the ball over a teammate's shoulder who is running in front of you.

Get two teammates to position themselves on each sideline, 3 to 5 meters from the centerline, diagonally facing each other with one ball. Position yourself on the same sideline as your teammate with the ball. Begin at the centerline and run straight along the line, looking back to receive a pass from your teammate. When you receive the ball, immediately pass it to your other teammate. Continue running to the opposite sideline, change directions, and receive another pass. Continue the drill in this manner for 30-second intervals, changing receivers at the end of each period.

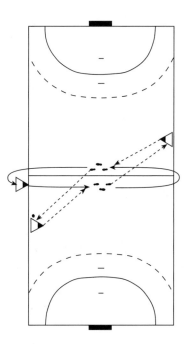

Success Goal = 10 complete passes in 30 seconds ___

Success Check
• Look back over your shoulder ___
• Catch the ball in stride___

To Increase Difficulty
• To make the angle more difficult for the receiver, move the passers closer to the centerline.

2. Primary Fast-Break Drill

The purpose of this drill is to practice running the floor properly and handling the long outlet pass. It also gives the goalie practice in throwing the long outlet pass to the wings and blocking the jump shot from the 6-meter line. Place a goalie in each goal. All players begin on one end, evenly distributed in the left and right wings, and each with a ball. Alternately, pass to the goalie and sprint straight to the centerline, receive a pass from the goalie and break toward the center of the goal. Dribble to the 6-meter line, jump into the area, and shoot (see Figure a). After shooting, remain behind the goal area. When all players have finished, form your lines in the wing positions and repeat the drill for six cycles. Receive 1 point for a completed pass and 1 point for a goal. Goalies compete against each other, receiving 1 point for a completed pass and 1 point for a blocked shot. Always run the same side of the court so you receive from the left and right wing positions.

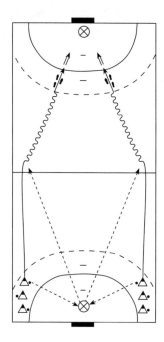

a. Long outlet pass directly to wing

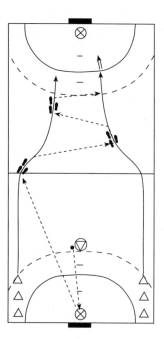

b. TO INCREASE DIFFICULTY: Long outlet pass and passing between wings

Success Goal =
a. Court Player:
   6 completed outlet passes ___
   6 goals scored ___
b. Goalie:
   Completed outlet passes ___
   Blocked shots ___

✔ Success Check
• Quick start—sprint ___
• Break to the middle near the centerline ___
• Goalie pass over the inside shoulder ___

To Increase Difficulty
• Coach stands at the 9-meter line and throws the ball to the goalie. Both the left and right wings sprint as soon as the ball leaves the coach's hand. Goalie throws the long outlet pass, players break toward the middle of the goal, passing the ball between themselves until one can approach the 6-meter line for a shot. No dribbling (see Figure b).
• Add a defender.

3. Secondary Fast-Break Drill: 3 vs. 2

The purpose of this drill is to practice the secondary break, moving the ball up the floor quickly and coordinating your movement tactically to beat defenders along the way. You and two team-mates start on the 6-meter line as shown in the diagram. Two other teammates position them-selves in front of the centerline to play defense. The defenders should only try to disrupt play around the centerline area and play only half speed. Place two markers on the centerline about 8 meters from each sideline. All action must stay between the sideline and the marker. Place a goalie in each goal with a supply of balls inside the goal. When the goalie says go, break from the 6-meter line, look for a short outlet pass from the goalie, and begin moving the ball quickly up the court. After beating the defenders at the centerline, finish the break by jumping into the goal area and shooting. Then move to the opposite side of the court and turn back toward the other goal. This time receive the outlet pass from the goalie and attempt to beat the defenders who have moved directly across the court behind the centerline. No dribbling is allowed. Make four consecutive trips down the floor. Earn 1 point for each time you beat the defense and don't drop the ball, and 1 point for scoring a goal. You can earn a total of 8 points.

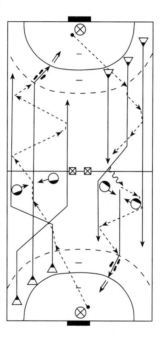

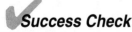**Success Goal** = 8 points earned ___

**To Increase Difficulty**
• Defense plays 100 percent.

**Success Check**
• Short, quick passes ___
• Coordinate movements tactically ___

4. Fast-Break: 6 vs. 6

The purpose of this drill is to practice the fast-break under gamelike circumstances. Designate two teams complete with goalkeepers. Your team begins on defense, setting up along the 6-meter line. The opposing team sets up an attack with three backcourts, two wings, and a circle runner. The attackers continuously attack and pass the ball around the defense from wing to wing. The defenders step out and shift as the ball is moved. When the coach blows the whistle, the attacker with the ball throws it hard to the goalie and everyone goes into transition. The goalie should knock the ball down, recover it, and look to initiate the fast-break. The fast-break team scores 1 point for a successful primary or secondary break. They keep possession until they miss a shot or a turnover or free-throw disrupts the break. If the defense successfully stops the fast-break, either by forcing a turnover, free-throw, or a missed or blocked shot, they receive 1 point and the teams switch roles. The game continues until either team scores 10 points.

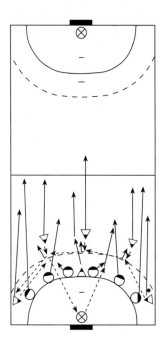

 **Success Goal** = First team to 10 points wins ___

✔ Success Check
- Wings break quickly ___
- Goalie decides quickly on long or short outlet ___
- Keep pressure on defenders—be tactical ___

To Decrease Difficulty
- Play 5 vs. 5 without a circle runner

5. Quick Retreat Drill: 2 vs. 2

The purpose of this drill is to practice player-to-player coverage in an effort to disrupt the momentum of the fast-break, which will allow teammates to get back and establish position. Get a partner to be your teammate and two other teammates to form another team. Place a goalie in the goal. The opposing players will be the attackers in the secondary break and position themselves along the 6-meter line with their backs to the goal. You and your partner will defend the break and stand opposite and facing them on the 9-meter line. When the goalie says "go," the attackers break out for a short outlet pass and try to move the ball quickly up the court against your team. Your job is to try to delay their attack between the 9-meter line and the centerline. Have your coach or teammate keep time with a stopwatch. Start the clock when the outlet pass is received. The attackers have 5 seconds to move the ball across the centerline. The defenders receive 1 point if they prevent the attackers from crossing within the time limit or disrupt the attack by forcing a turnover or free-throw. The attackers receive 1 point if they move the ball across the centerline within the time limit. Teams switch attack and defense after each point.

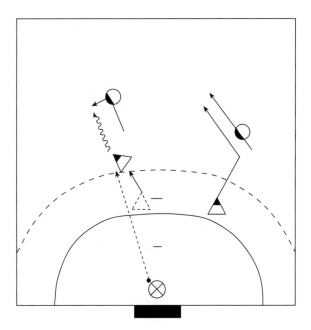

 **Success Goal** = First team to 10 points wins ___

Success Check
• Pressure player-to-player defense ___

6. Half-Court Pick-Up Drill: 4 vs. 4

The purpose of this quick retreat drill is to practice organizing a temporary barrier in front of the goal and trying to prevent high-percentage shots. Form two teams of four court players and a goalie. You and your teammates set up on defense around the centerline. The other team sets up between the 9-meter and 6-meter lines ready to fast-break. Their goalie in the goal area with a ball is ready to make an outlet pass. The goalie makes a short outlet pass to an attacker and they attempt to complete a fast-break. Your team's job on defense is to quickly force them into an error, or retreat quickly to set up your barrier in front of the goal and attempt to keep them from scoring. The attackers receive 1 point for a goal, and the defenders receive 1 point if they stop them, including a missed shot or goalie save.

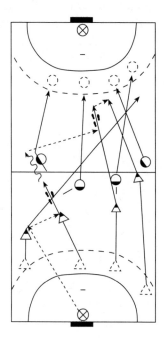

Success Goal = First team to 5 points wins ___

To Increase Difficulty
• Play five attackers against four defenders.

Success Check
• Try to force a quick error ___
• Protect high-percentage shot areas—force action to the wings ___

TRANSITIONS SUCCESS SUMMARY

Your team's ability to swiftly move from defense to attack and quickly retreat from attack to defense plays a big role in how you compete over the course of a contest. Because of the fast pace of team handball, transitions are numerous and consequently an important part of the game. Consistent, effective use of the primary and secondary fast-breaks provides quick scoring and wears down the opposition both physically and psychologically. Immediate reaction to the loss of ball possession by a quick retreat to defense prevents these results from happening to your team. Spending time practicing transitions will help build confidence on defense and add a dynamic dimension to your team's attack.

STEP 11

TEAM ATTACK: SUPPORT POINTS

T he legendary football coach Knute Rockne said, "The secret of winning football games is working more as a team, less as individuals." The same secret applies to creating a successful attack in team handball.

Fundamental team handball attack organizes all six court players in an attack system called "support points." Support points consists of moving the ball quickly and accurately from one player to the next, providing the continuity and security necessary to carry out group tactics spontaneously. Get your team together to practice the essential elements of support points: positioning, passing, and patience. Your team will also learn how to attack in special situations.

Why Is Team Attack Important?

If the fast-break doesn't result in a score, you and your teammates must settle into an organized attack. From this point you must collectively focus your efforts against the set defense to score. This is not to say that one-on-one efforts are discouraged. Certainly you should pursue such actions at the proper times and circumstances. But over the course of a game, an organized team attack is more effective simply because it increases the number of scoring options.

Positioning in Support Points

Team attack begins from a basic formation, which is simply the starting positions players take based on their skills and abilities. The formation provides organization and balance but doesn't prohibit players' creativity or freedom of movement. Figures 11.1a and b show two basic attack formations, the 3-3 and the 2-4. The 3-3 formation is ideal for support points because the equal spacing of players across the backcourt allows shorter passes and better ball control.

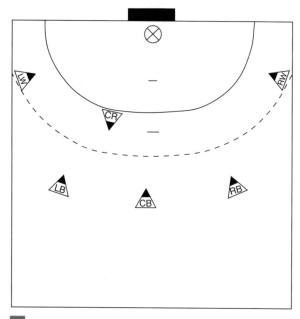

Figure 11.1a The 3-3 formation.

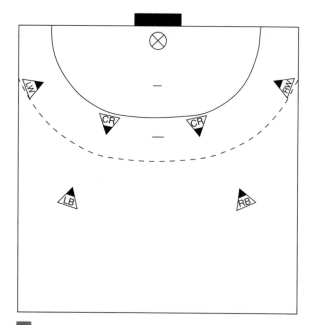

Figure 11.1b The 2-4 formation.

Each position in the attack formation has specific physical, technical, and psychological requirements. Following are characteristics that you should possess to play each position.

Backcourts

The backcourt players initiate most attack combinations, so your play significantly influences how well the team performs. You must be a good playmaker and ballhandler, able to coordinate with the actions of teammates and make good decisions quickly. You must be a strong, accurate set shooter and jump shooter. It is obvious that the ability to score from long range (9 to 11 meters) directly contributes to the attack, but it contributes indirectly also. Quality backcourt shooting forces defenders to step out farther, which extends the depth of the defense and creates more open space for the wings and circle runner. Height can be an advantage in the backcourt to help you see and shoot over the defense. It is advantageous if you play on the opposite side of the court of your throwing arm, so your power is toward the middle of the court. If you are right handed you should play in the left backcourt, and if left handed in the right backcourt, so that your power is toward the middle of the court (see Figure 11.2).

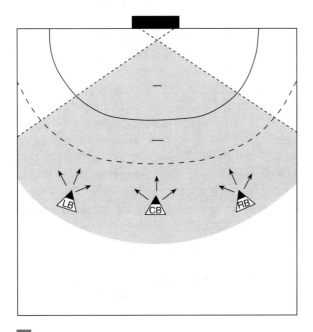

Figure 11.2 Backcourt movement area.

Wings

Because of the limited playing area and difficult shooting angle, the wing position is highly specialized. You need to be quick and an accomplished faker, able to play one-on-one. Speed and the ability to pass and catch on the run are important because you lead the fast-break. Agility and good jumping ability are essential for you to create a good shooting position from a difficult angle (see Figure 11.3).

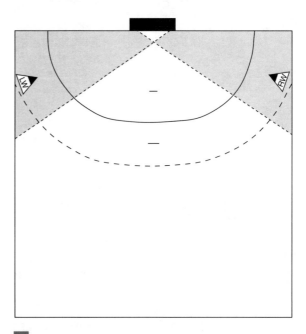

Figure 11.3 Wing movement area.

Circle Runner

You've heard the phrase "playing in the trenches" referring to football linemen. That's how it is playing circle runner; you work in the thick of the defense to create opportunities for the big scorers. As a circle runner, more than any attacker, you need to understand that contact is part of the game. A cool head and tactical discipline will help you stay focused and undisturbed by the unceasing physical encounters with defenders. Strength and a good sense of balance are important for withstanding the physical demands of playing circle runner. You need to possess excellent catching skill and be able to handle the ball in traffic along the 6-meter line (see Figure 11.4).

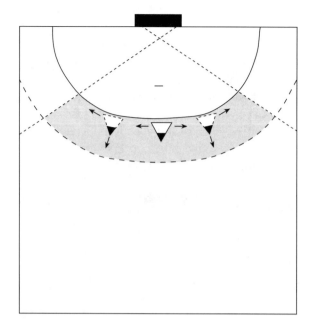

Figure 11.4 Circle runner movement area.

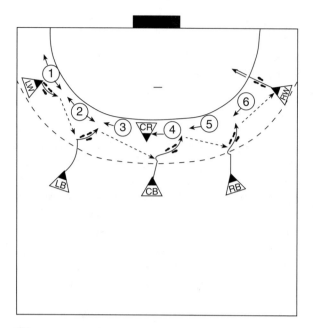

Figure 11.5 Support points.

Passing in Support Points

Moving the ball from wing to wing with quick, accurate passes is the second key to support points. Execution of the piston movement is very important. For support points to be effective, each player must be a threat to the defense. When you receive the ball, attack the gap aggressively. If the gap closes, pass quickly to the next attacker who has moved into position to support you. This attacker continues attacking in the same manner, until there is a clear scoring opportunity. As the ball is passed around the defense wall several times, the attackers develop a rhythmic movement that looks like a piston moving forward and backward. This is how support points provides continuity to the attack. Quick passing and aggressive attacking force defenders to step out, help, recover, and eventually become out of position creating an overload.

While moving the ball in support points, you may use any of the offensive combinations. The backcourts may use crossing at any time. The circle runner constantly looks to help by setting picks for the backcourts and by moving along the 6-meter line into openings behind the defense. The wings must play patiently to effectively contribute to the attack. They coordinate with the backcourts to initiate support points by attacking the gap, and if the overload presents itself, finish support points with a strong shot (see Figure 11.5).

Patience in Support Points

Wait for a good scoring opportunity. If support points is accompanied by patience the defense will eventually make mistakes, allowing openings in the defense for drives to the 6-meter line and open shots. Don't rush to complete the attack. Keep in mind that when your team has the ball your opponents cannot score, so work patiently for a high-percentage shot. Taking a poor-percentage shot, which the goalie or defenders can easily block, denies your team a potential goal and turns the ball over to your opponents for a chance to score. When there is a good scoring opportunity, be quick, decisive, and determined to put the ball in the goal. The bottom line is that the best possible positioning, the most precise passing, and the most enduring patience are of little value if there is not a great desire to finish the attack when the opportunity arises.

Points to Remember in Support Points:

- Move the ball with short, quick passes.
- Run to receive and play in good timing with teammates.
- Attack the gap.
- Be a threat.
- Don't let the defense tie you up (avoid free-throws).
- Be alert and support teammates when playing without the ball.
- Be patient.

Special Situations

Most of the game is played in numerical equality, and you should focus most of your tactical preparation on this. However, during a 2-minute suspension you will attack with a numerical advantage or disadvantage, and these periods can be turning points of the game. Following are some tactical suggestions for playing in these situations.

Attacking 6 vs. 5:

■ Don't rush the attack. The objective is to score one goal during the two minutes of the suspension.

■ Work patiently for a high-percentage shot.

■ Use support points to take advantage of the natural overload of 6 vs. 5.

■ Play with two circle runners (2-4 formation) to create more openings on the 6-meter line (see Figure 11.6).

Attacking 5 vs. 6:

■ Play with discipline and caution. The objective is to protect the ball and keep possession until the suspended player returns. However, running time off the clock without attempting to score is called passive play or stalling. The passive play call is based entirely on the judgment of the referee and results in a free-throw.

■ To keep pressure on the defense, continually attack the gaps trying to break through to the 6-meter line. This action will also help your team draw more free-throws, which eat time off the 2-minute suspension and prevent a passive play call. Shoot only if there is a clear opportunity to score.

■ To increase ball control, play with three backcourts, two wings, and no circle runner (see Figure 11.7).

■ Always be in a position to support a teammate with the ball.

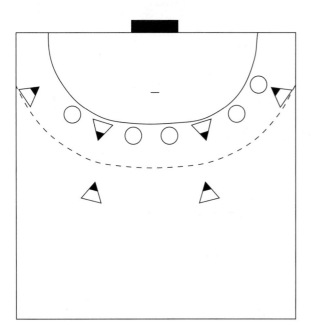

Figure 11.6 Attacking 6 vs. 5—2-4 formation.

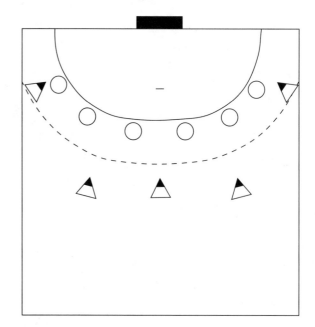

Figure 11.7 Attacking 5 vs. 6—no circle runner.

TEAM ATTACK

DRILLS

1. The Shell Drill: 3-3 Formation

The purpose of this drill is to develop your team's competence and confidence in support points. It will also help you develop the ability to incorporate all tactics while moving the ball in support points. Set up in the 3-3 formation without a circle runner, just three backcourts and two wings. (1) Start support points in the left wing, move the ball around to the right wing and back to the left wing, who finishes support points with a wing shot. Alternate starting and finishing in each wing. Perform three shots from each wing (see Figure a). (2) Start support points in the left wing, move the ball around to the right wing and back to the center backcourt, who crosses with the left backcourt for a jump shot. To alternate crossing with each backcourt, alternate starting in each wing. Perform three crosses in each backcourt (see Figure b). (3) Now add the circle runner. Start support points in the left wing, move the ball around to the right wing, and as the ball comes back across, the circle runner plays pick and roll with the left backcourt. Alternate starting in each wing so the circle runner can alternate pick and roll with the left backcourt and right backcourt. Perform three pick and rolls with each BC (see Figure c). Your goal is to handle the ball without error and finish each tactic with a score.

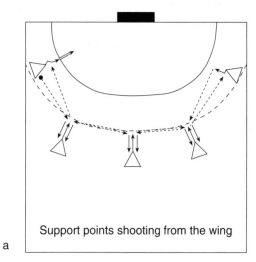

a

Support points shooting from the wing

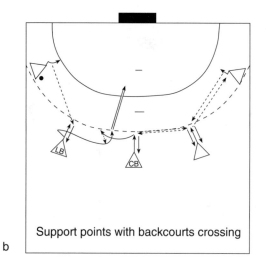

b

Support points with backcourts crossing

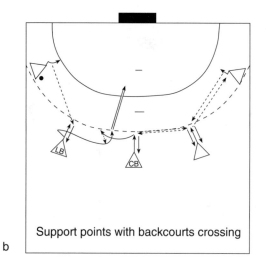

c

Support points with pick and roll

Success Goal = 6 successful support points—score from the wing ___
6 successful support points—score from crossing ___
6 successful support points—score from pick and roll ___

Success Check
• Ball control ___
• Timely execution ___
• Finish the attack ___

2. Half-Court Scrimmage: 6 vs. 6

The purpose of this drill is to practice team attack in a gamelike situation. You and five teammates form a team and organize your attack in the 3-3 formation. Six other teammates form a defensive wall along the 6-meter line. Scrimmage for 10 minutes with your coach as referee and scorekeeper. The defense scores 1 point each time they win possession of the ball and 2 points for scoring on a fast-break. Your attacking team scores 1 point for each of the following: (a) successful execution of overload in support points—score an additional point for a goal, (b) successful execution of crossing—score an additional point for a goal, (c) successful execution of pick and roll—score an additional point for a goal.

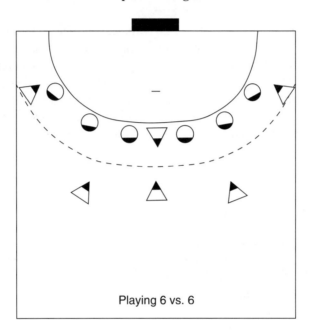

Playing 6 vs. 6

Success Goal = Team that scores the most points wins

Attacking team's score ____

Defensive team's score ____

Success Check
• Read the defense ____
• Make good decisions ____
• Finish the attack ____

TEAM ATTACK SUCCESS SUMMARY

Good team attack involves all six players combining their efforts to score goals. Support points is the most important procedure in team attack because it provides your team the continuity and security necessary to execute your tactics consistently. The 3-3 formation, consisting of three backcourts, two wings, and a circle runner, is ideal for support points. The equal spacing of players gives balance to the attack and allows for shorter passes and better control. The key to support points is passing the ball quickly from wing to wing, using the piston movement and attacking the gap aggressively. Incorporate small group tactics as the rhythm of support points builds. Don't rush to complete the attack. Work patiently for a high-percentage shot. If support points is accompanied by a lot of patience, the defense will eventually make mistakes and a good scoring opportunity will present itself.

STEP 12

TEAM DEFENSE: THE 6-0 ZONE

The main menu on a computer is your gateway to many other options. The 6-0 zone defense in team handball is your team's starting point and the gateway to other more advanced defensive formations.

When practicing the 6-0 zone defense, you and your teammates will learn to "count," to understand the defensive concepts of width, depth, and density along with player positioning and overall coverage. You will also explore some special defensive situations.

Why Is Team Defense Important?

Even though defense is less spectacular than offense, it is no less vital to your team achieving good results. In fact, team success is highly dependent on the ability to prevent goals. Scoring goals is important, but if you give up a goal for every one you score you gain nothing. Any team is going to have occasional off games in attack, but this should never happen on the defensive end of the floor. Strong defense is the one aspect of play that you should be able to count on every game because, more than anything else, it requires effort and attitude. There is no doubt that effective defense relies on each player mastering individual skills and tactics, but the key is how well they can weave these into a cohesive unit with a strong personality of its own. Each player develops this through a desire to excel and a sense of responsibility to the team. Playing defense is hard work and provides little immediate gratification like that of scoring a goal. In the long run, however, the boost in confidence and morale that strong, consistent defensive play gives your team is invaluable.

The 6-0 Zone Defense

In handball, zone defenses are most effective against an organized set attack. The zone is established in front of and close to the goal area. The defenders'

positions relative to the 6-meter line determine the classification of zone defense. The 6-0 zone has six players on the 6-meter line and zero players out front. Examples of other defenses are the 5-1, 4-2, and 3-2-1. All zone defenses are named by counting the number of players from the 6-meter line out (see Figures 12.1a-d).

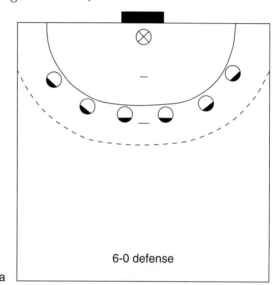

a   6-0 defense

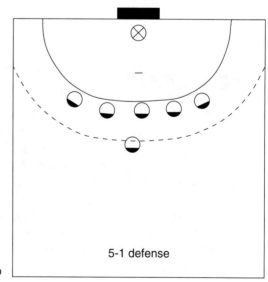

b   5-1 defense

142

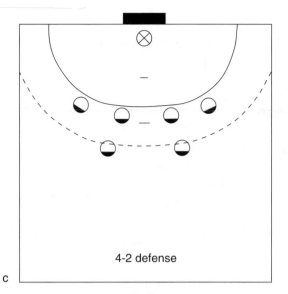

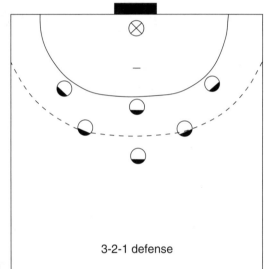

Figure 12.1a-d Four zone defenses.

The 6-0 zone involves all six defenders moving as a unit, forming a movable wall that maintains its greatest strength between the ball and the goal. The zone's effectiveness relies heavily on how well defenders control their defensive space and assist each other by executing the help triangle. A sound understanding of the 6-0 defense provides the foundation to use more complex defensive systems. Adhering to the following guidelines will help you learn and properly execute the 6-0 defense.

Counting

To help define each defender's defensive space and individual responsibilities within the zone, a num-

bering and counting system is used. The basic position for all defenders in the 6-0 zone is along the 6-meter line. The defenders are numbered from the sideline to the middle of the court. The defenders next to the sideline, usually the wings, are numbered 1 and are responsible for the players on the outside of the attack. The players next to the number 1 defenders are numbered 2 and are responsible for the second players in attack, usually a backcourt or a circle runner. The middle defenders are numbered 3 and are responsible for the third players in from the outside of the attack, usually the center backcourt or a circle runner. Each defender takes responsibility for one player at a time. Even when the offense is not so neatly organized, you can still determine assignments by counting from the wings on both sides (see Figure 12.2).

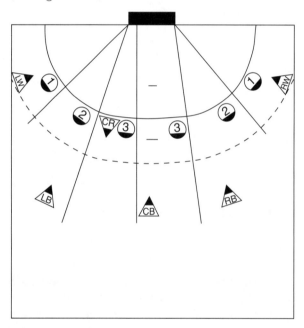

Figure 12.2 Counting.

Achieving Width, Depth, and Density in the 6-0 Defense

Zone defenses consist of three elements: width is the area covered along the 6-meter line providing protection of the goal area; depth is the area covered out from the 6-meter line providing defense of backcourt shots; and density is the close proximity of defenders minimizing the chance for attackers to drive to the 6-meter line. No one zone meets all these requirements automatically. The 6-0 zone has natural width and density, but not depth. Depth is achieved by playing aggressively and stepping out to meet attacks from the backcourt at the 9-meter line (see Figure 12.3). After the attacker passes the ball to a teammate, you should break contact and recover to the 6-meter line to maintain density, as the next defender steps out to meet the continuing attack, and so on. Remember that you must form a help triangle every time a defender steps out (see Step 9).

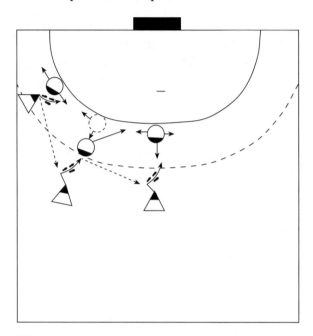

Figure 12.3 Creating depth by stepping out.

Player Positioning

The positioning of individual players in the zone is important in helping fulfill the width, depth, and density of the defense. Here are some guidelines to follow when selecting players for each defensive position.

Most teams direct their attack actions toward the high-percentage scoring area in the middle of the court. Tall and strong number 3 defenders provide excellent shot blocking and defense. This will provide excellent shot blocking and circle runner defense. Players occupying the number 2 positions must be strong enough to defend a circle runner, but quick and agile enough to defend a faking and driving backcourt player. Height and strength are not determining factors for playing the number 1 defensive positions. Quickness and lateral mobility are necessary to defend the one-on-one moves of the wings.

Coverage

The zone is constantly adjusting to the position of both the ball and the attackers. As the defense shifts, each defender should keep in his or her field of vision the ball and the player in his or her defensive space. As the ball moves farther away from your space, you can give more distance between yourself and your opponent. Doing this helps keep the density of the zone and prevents gaps. How much distance is safe? You should be able to close the distance before your opponent can receive a direct pass from a teammate (see Figure 12.4).

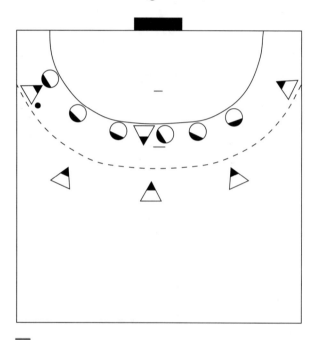

Figure 12.4 Shifting to keep the density of the defense in the area of the ball.

The defense must be careful not to overshift with the ball and leave any attackers unaccounted for. It's important to count and make sure there is one defender matched to one attacker at all times. If a defender notices that there is no attacker in his or her defensive space, then an overload has been created and a teammate is covering two attackers. The key to avoiding this is counting and communicating so the defense can continually adjust to proper coverage (see Figures 12.5a and b).

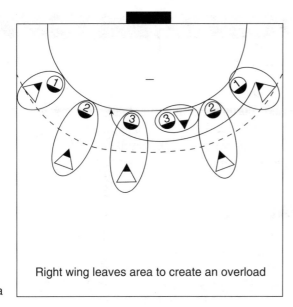

Right wing leaves area to create an overload

a

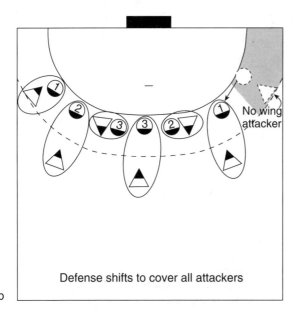

No wing attacker

Defense shifts to cover all attackers

b

Figure 12.5a-b Adjusting defensive coverage for an overload situation.

Special Situations

There are some defensive situations that may occur in a game that warrant special consideration because they either pose a period of vulnerability or provide a time for extra opportunity. These situations occur because either team has been issued a 2-minute suspension. Following are two such situations and tactical suggestions for dealing with them.

Defending with numerical advantage: six defenders versus five attackers

■ Play more aggressively, try to force mistakes.
■ Defend player to player against the best shooter while the rest of the team stays in 5-0 zone.

Defending with numerical disadvantage: five defenders versus six attackers

■ Requires increased individual and collective effort.
■ Play a 5-0 zone, and do not step out; make an extra effort to block backcourt shots. Keep the zone dense, with special attention to protecting the high-percentage shooting area in front of the goal.
■ Force the action of the attackers to the lower-percentage shooting area in the wing.

Player-to-Player Defense

You may be wondering why player-to-player defense has not been mentioned. First of all, player-to-player defense must be flawlessly executed to present a big problem for a fast and varied attack. This requires that each defender has not only a high level of technical and tactical ability but also a high level of physical conditioning because of the large playing court. Player-to-player defense is risky and puts great demand on players over the course of a game, which could ultimately affect other areas of performance. Although difficult to employ as a primary defense, there are certain situations when it would be appropriate:

1. To apply pressure when your team is 6 vs. 5 during a 2-minute suspension.
2. When you are playing a team that is poorly conditioned and has weak skills.
3. To try to force the action and get quick possession of the ball when you are behind late in the game.

TEAM DEFENSE

DRILLS

1. 6-0 Shell Drill

The purpose of this drill is to practice shifting and coordinating movements in the 6-0 zone. You and five teammates position yourselves in the 6-0 defense. Position six teammates in the 3-3 attack formation, with the circle runner playing stationary between the number 3 defenders. As the attackers pass the ball in support points, the defenders shift with the ball, executing the help triangle and covering the circle runner at all times.

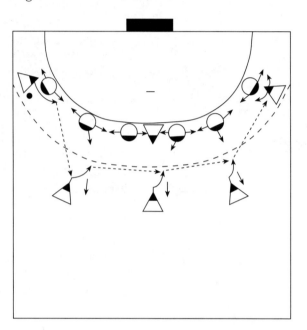

Success Goal = 30 seconds of proper positioning in the 6-0 zone ___

✔**Success Check**
• Shift with the ball ___
• Form help triangle on the ball ___
• Cover the circle runner at all times ___

To Increase Difficulty
• Play with seven attackers and position a circle runner between the number 2 and number 3 defenders on each side.
• Increase drill by 10-second increments up to 60 seconds.

To Decrease Difficulty
• Eliminate the circle runner.

2. Half-Court Scrimmage: 6 vs. 6

The purpose of this drill is to practice the 6-0 zone, incorporating all defensive tactics, in a game-like situation. You and five teammates form a team and set up on defense in the 6-0 zone. Six other teammates form an attacking team and set up in the 3-3 formation. Position a goalie in the goal. Scrimmage for 10 minutes with your coach as referee and scorekeeper. The attackers score 2 points for scoring a goal or 1 point for getting off a shot that is blocked by the goalie. Your defending team scores 1 point for each of the following: (a) successfully defending a crossing, (b) successfully defending a pick and roll, (c) intercepting a pass, (d) scoring on a fast-break after a goalie save, and (e) keeping the attackers from getting off a shot on goal in 45 seconds.

Success Goal = Team that scores the most points wins

Defensive team's score ___
Attacking team's score ___

Success Check

• Shift as a unit—be like a movable wall ___
• Communicate with teammates ___
• Count to cover overload situations ___
• Create depth by stepping out ___

TEAM DEFENSE SUCCESS SUMMARY

When you begin working on a computer you start your explorations from the main menu. The 6-0 zone defense is recommended for beginning teams because it is the main menu of all the defensive principles. All zone defenses consist of three elements: width, depth, and density, but no one defense meets all these elements automatically. The 6-0 zone positions players in the zone to take advantage of individual strengths and to allow the best incorporation of small group tactics. The 6-0 zone defense is the most effective against an organized set attack. Your team establishes the 6-0 zone in front of the goal area and simulates a moveable human wall that maintains its greatest strength between the ball and the goal. Team success is highly dependent on strong defense. Your team's ability to consistently prevent good scoring opportunities for the opposition builds confidence and morale, and these intangibles positively affect all aspects of performance.

RATING YOUR PROGRESS

At this point you have been exposed to individual fundamental skills used in game play as well as tactics and strategies used by a small group or the entire team. The following rating chart allows you to rate your overall progress. Rate your success in team handball by writing a number in the space to the right of each skill listed. Read each item carefully and respond objectively. Then, review your strengths and weaknesses, and set new goals. Share your knowledge and expertise with other players willing and eager to learn.

Rating Points

5 = Outstanding

4 = Very good

3 = Fair

2 = Needs extra work

1 = Weakness

Individual Fundamental Skills

Passing and catching:
    Overhand pass___
    Wrist pass___
    Catching the ball___
    Catching above the waist___
    Catching below the waist___
    Catching while running___

Attacking:
    Three actions of the piston movement:
        1. Run to receive___
        2. Use three steps___
        3. Back up quickly___
    Side-stepping___

Dribbling:
    Alone on fast-break___
    One-on-one___
    Avoid 3-second violation___

Shooting:
    Set shot___
    Jump shot___
    Wing shot___
    Fall shot___
    7-meter throw___

Individual defensive skills:
    Basic defensive stance___
    Checking—making contact___
    Blocking shots___
        Set shot___
        Jump shot___

Goalkeeping:
    Knowledge___
    Special rules___

Mental game:
    Confidence___
    Courage___
    Composure___
    Leadership___

Blocking shots:
    Blocking high shots___
    Blocking low shots___
    Blocking medium shots___
    Blocking wing shots___
    Recovering the ball___
    Initiating the fast-break___

Game Concept Skills

Individual attack tactics:
    Anticipation___
    Maintain ball possession___
    Use fakes___
    Read the defense___

Individual defense tactics:
    Defensive space___
    Stepping out___
    Recovering to basic position___

Overload principle:
    Support attacking teammate___
    Crossing___
    Pick___
    Pick and roll___

Defense triangle:
    Stepping out on point___
    Squeezing in___
    Communication___

Take over–pass on___
Guarding the circle runner___
Switching___

Team Play

Transitions—offense:
    1. Primary fast-break___
       Goalie pass___
       Wing breaking___
    2. Secondary fast-break___
       Spacing___
       Depth___

Transitions—defense:
    Quick retreat___
    Pressure the ball___
    Hustle back___
    Organize the zone___
    Communication___

Team attack:
    Support points___
    Positioning___
    Passing___
    Patience___

Attacking 6 vs. 5___
Attacking 5 vs. 6___

Team defense:
    Zone defense___
    Player-to-player defense___
    6-0 defense___
    Counting___
    Width, depth, density___
    Player positions___
    Coverage___

Defending 6 vs. 5___
Defending 5 vs. 6___

APPENDIX A: TEAM HANDBALL SIMPLIFIED RULES

This is a simplified rules handout. If you have any questions about specific rules, please refer to the International Handball Federation official rule book. Rule books can be purchased from the U.S. Team Handball Federation, One Olympic Plaza, Colorado Springs, CO 80909, phone number 719-578-4582.

1. **The Playing Court.** 20 meters (65' 7") by 40 meters (131' 3"). The goal area line, or 6-meter line (19' 8"), is probably the most important line. *No one except the goalie is allowed to stand in the goal area.* The goal opening is 2 meters by 3 meters. Players may jump into the area if the ball is released before landing in the area. The court is larger than a basketball court, but the length may be shortened when space is limited (see Figure A1).

2. **The Ball.**
   - 32-Panel Leather Ball:
     Women's = 54 to 56 centimeters, 325 to 400 grams
     Men's = 58 to 60 centimeters, 425 to 475 grams
   - Airfilled Foam Ball—"SuperSafe Elite" by *Sportime* (1-800-283-5700). Handball (350g), Junior Handball (320g), Mini-Handball (270g)

3. **Number of Players.** Seven players on each team = six court players + one goalie (see Figure A2). Maximum of twelve players may dress and participate in a game for each team. Substitutes may enter game at anytime through own substitution area as long as the player they are replacing has left the court.

4. **Uniform of the Players.** Players' numbers = 1 to 20; shirts and shorts are the same color. Goalkeeper must wear different color shirt from teammates and opponents. No jewelry.

5. **Referees.** Two: court referee and goal line referee; referees have complete authority—decisions are final. The referees are assisted by a timer and scorer.

6. **Duration of the Game.** For 18 years and over: 2 x 30 minutes—10-minute halftime. Tournaments and youth: 2 x 15 minutes or 2 x 20 minutes. Running time except for injury and one team time-out per half.

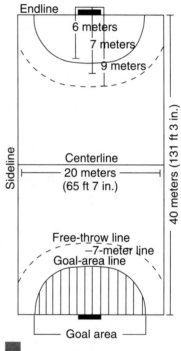

Figure A1 The playing court.

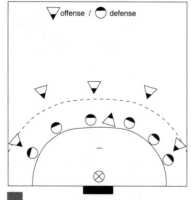

Figure A2 Offense vs. defense.

Change benches at halftime. Game ends in a tie unless game demands a winner. (Overtime: 2 x 5 minutes.)

Passive play: It is illegal to keep the ball in a team's possession without making a recognizable attempt to attack and try to score. In other words, a team cannot stall (free-throw awarded for opponents).

7. **Throw-off.** Taken by the team that wins the coin toss and chooses to start the game with the ball. Each team must be in its own half of court with the defense 3 meters away from the ball. Following a whistle, the ball is passed from center court to a teammate and play begins. Throw-off is repeated *after every goal scored and after half-time* (see Figure A3).

8. **Scoring.** Goal is scored when entire ball crosses goal line inside the goal. Goal may be scored from any throw (i.e., free-throw, throw-in, throw-off, goal-throw).

9. **Playing the Ball.**
   Player is allowed to:
   • Run with the ball 3 steps (violation is a free-throw)
   • Hold the ball 3 seconds (violation is a free-throw)
   • Unlimited dribble with 3 steps allowed before and after dribbling (no double dribble)

   Player is *not* allowed to:
   • Endanger an opponent with the ball
   • Pull, hit, or punch the ball out of the hands of an opponent
   • Contact the ball below the knee
   • Dive on the floor for a rolling or stationary ball

10. **Defending the Opponent.** A player is allowed to use the torso of the body to obstruct an opponent with or without the ball. However, using the outstretched arms or legs to obstruct, push, hold, trip, or hit is *not* allowed. The attacking player is not allowed to charge into a defensive player (free-throw awarded).

11. **Throw-in.** Awarded when ball goes out of bounds on the sideline or when the ball is last touched by a defensive player (excluding the goalie) and goes out of bounds over the endline. The throw-in is taken from the spot where the ball crossed the sideline, or if it crossed the endline, from the nearest corner. The thrower must place one foot on the sideline to execute the throw. All opposing players must stay 3 meters away from the ball.

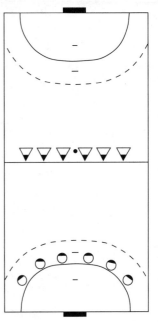

Figure A3 Throw-off.

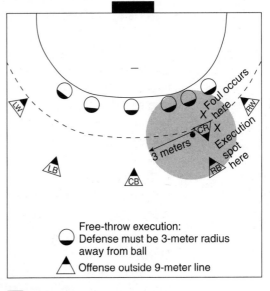

Figure A4 Free-throw execution.

12. **Referee Throw.**
    Awarded when:
    - The ball touches anything above the court
    - Simultaneous infringement of the rules
    - Simultaneous possession

    Referee throws the ball vertically between two opposing players. Players jumping may grab the ball or tap it to a teammate. All other players must be 3 meters away from the throw. Time-out is called and the referee throw is always taken at center court.

13. **Free-Throw.** For a minor foul or violation, a free-throw is awarded to the opponents at the exact spot it took place. If the foul or violation occurs between the goal area line and the 9-meter line, the throw is taken from the nearest point outside the 9-meter line. All players on the team taking the free-throw must be *outside* the 9-meter line. Opponents must be 3 meters away from the ball when the throw is taken. The thrower must keep one foot in contact with the floor, then pass or shoot (see Figure A4).

14. **7-Meter Throw.**
    Awarded when:
    - A foul destroys a clear chance to score a goal
    - The goalie carries the ball back into his or her own goal area
    - A court player intentionally plays the ball to his or her own goalie in the goal area and the goalie touches the ball
    - A defensive player enters his or her goal area to gain advantage over an attacking player in possession of the ball

    All players must be outside the free-throw line when the throw is taken. Player taking throw has 3 seconds to shoot after referee whistles. Any player may take the 7-meter throw (see Figure A5).

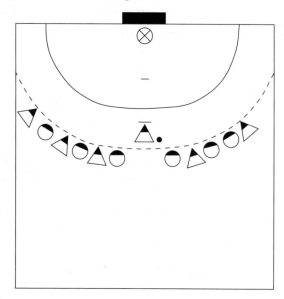

Figure A5   The 7-meter throw execution.

15. **Goal-Throw.**
    Awarded when:
    - The ball rebounds off the goalkeeper over the endline
    - The ball is thrown over the endline by the attacking team

    Goalie takes the throw inside the goal area and is not restricted by the 3-step/3-second rule.

16. **Progressive Punishments.** Fouls that require more punishment than just a free-throw. "Actions" directed mainly at the opponent and not the ball are to be punished progressively (e.g., reaching around, holding, pushing, hitting, tripping, or jumping into opponent). See the referee signals in Figure A6.

    Warnings (yellow card)
    Referee gives only one warning to a player for rule violations and a total of three to a team. Exceeding these limits results in 2-minute suspensions thereafter. Warnings are not required prior to giving a 2-minute suspension.

2-minute suspension

Awarded for:

- Serious or repeated rule violations
- Unsportsmanlike conduct
- Illegal substitution

The suspended player's team plays short for 2 minutes.

Disqualification and Exclusion (red card)

Disqualification = three 2-minute suspensions; disqualified player must leave court and bench but team may replace the player after the 2-minute suspension expires.

Exclusion = given for assault; excluded player's team continues short one player for rest of the game.

REFEREE SIGNALS

The referee does not handle the ball on any foul or violation. The player retrieves the ball and puts it into play as quickly as possible. The referee uses hand signals to explain calls and to indicate the direction the ball will be moving when put in play.

ENTERING THE GOAL AREA	ILLEGAL CATCHING, BOUNCING, OR FUMBLING	TOO MANY STEPS OR HOLDING THE BALL TOO LONG	HOLDING AND PUSHING	STRIKING ON THE ARM
ATTACKER FAULT RUNNING INTO, JUMPING INTO	THROW-IN	GOAL-THROW	FREE-THROW (DIRECTION)	KEEP THE DISTANCE OF 3 METERS
TIME WASTING	GOAL	REFEREE-THROW	REFEREE-THROW EXECUTION	WARNING (YELLOW) DISQUALIFICATION (RED)
SUSPENSION (2-MINUTES)	EXCLUSION	TIME-OUT	PERMISSION TO ENTER THE COURT	PERMISSION FOR SUBSTITUTE GOAL-KEEPER TO ENTER THE COURT AFTER TIME-OUT

 Figure A6

PPENDIX B: MARKING A TEAM HANDBALL COURT

Many gyms are not big enough to accommodate a regulation team handball court. If this is the case in your facility, here are some guidelines for converting your floor space and a key for converting meters to feet.

1. Determine the maximum length and width of the court that you can set up. *Remember to include a 1-meter safety zone along both sidelines and a 2-meter safety zone on both ends.*

2. Put down two parallel sidelines to the allowable length, not to exceed 40 meters.

3. Measure and mark the center point of both sidelines. Put down the centerline by connecting these two center points.

4. Put down two parallel endlines to the allowable width, not to exceed 20 meters. Make sure the outer goal lines (endlines) are perpendicular to the sidelines.

5. Measure and mark the center point of both outer goal lines (endlines).

6. Measure and place a mark one and one-half meters from the center of goal line in both directions. These marks are the focal points for preparing the goal-area (6-meter) line and the free-throw (9-meter) line and are the location of the goalposts. (See Figure B1a.)

7. Measure and mark a quarter-circle arc from each focal point for the goal-area and free-throw lines (see Figure B1b). Starting at one focal point (where one goalpost will be), tape the end of a measuring tape or 6-meter string to the floor. Extend the string straight out in front of the focal point (90-degree angle to the goal line).

8. Hold a piece of chalk at the 6-meter mark and make a quarter-circle arc to the outer goal line keeping the string tight. Repeat this at the other focal point (where the other goalpost will be).

9. Join the two quarter circles with a 3-meter straight line directly in front of the goal.

10. Go over the chalk marking with 5-centimeter-wide gym floor tape following along the curve and trying to avoid wrinkles.

11. Repeat the process for the 9-meter line but use pieces of tape 15 centimeters long instead of continuous tape.

12. Returning to the goal line center point, measure and mark directly in front of the goal the 4-meter goalkeeper's restraining line and the 7-meter line. The goalie's line is 15 centimeters long and the 7-meter line 1 meter long.

13. Measure and mark the substitution area lines on the sideline where the team benches and official's table are located. The substitution lines are 4.45 meters from the center line and are 30 centimeters long. Fifteen centimeters extends into the court and 15 centimeters extends off the court.

14. Move the goals into place on the goal line. The inside back corner of the goalpost is placed on the previously marked focal points. Increase the width of the actual goal line to the width of the goalposts. This line will extend 3 centimeters *into the goal area.*

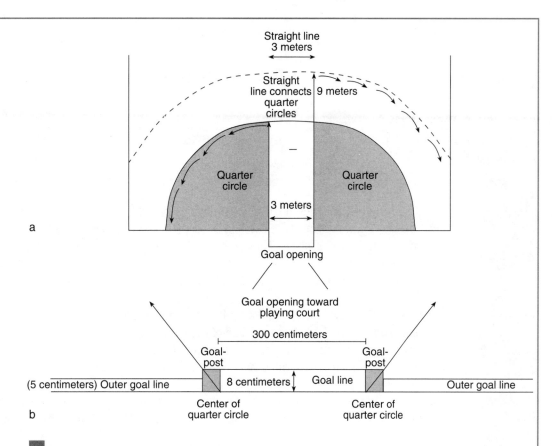

Straight line
3 meters

Straight
line connects
quarter
circles

9 meters

Quarter
circle

Quarter
circle

3 meters

Goal opening

a

Goal opening toward
playing court

300 centimeters

Goal-
post

Goal-
post

(5 centimeters) Outer goal line

8 centimeters

Goal line

Outer goal line

Center of
quarter circle

Center of
quarter circle

b

■ **Figure B1a-b** Marking the court.

Team Handball Markings	Metric	U.S. Equivalent
Width of court lines:	5 centimeter (cm)	2 inches (in.)
Width of goalpost/goal line:	8 cm	3-1/8 in.
Length of free-throw dashes:	15 cm	6 in.
Length of black/white goal face spaces:	20 cm	8 in.
Black upper corners of goal face:	28 cm	11-1/8 in.
Length of penalty line:	1 meter (m)	3 feet (ft) 3-3/8 in.
Height of goal opening:	2 m	6 ft 6-3/4 in.
Width of goal opening:	3 m	9 ft 10-1/8 in.
Goalie restriction line:	4 m	13 ft 1-1/2 in.
Each substitution area:	4.45 m	14 ft 7-3/4 in.
Goal-area line:	6 m	19 ft 8-1/4 in.
Penalty line:	7 m	22 ft 11-5/8 in.
Free-throw line:	9 m	29 ft 6-3/8 in.
Width of court:	20 m	65 ft 7-3/8 in.
Length of court:	40 m	131 ft 2-3/4 in.

GLOSSARY

attack—A team or individual tries to score when they are in possession of the ball.

centerline—The line divides the court in the center, and the game begins at the centerline.

charging—An offensive player runs into or over a stationary defensive player who is in proper position.

checking—Body contact between attacker and defender with the torso and limbs as permitted by the rules.

circle—The nickname for the goal-area line or 6-meter line.

depth of court—The longitudinal scope of the court from endline to endline.

endline—This is another term for the outer goal line.

free-throw—This term describes how the ball is put back into play after a minor rule violation. The opponents maintain 3 meters from the player taking the free-throw.

free-throw line—The dashed line at 9 meters used for taking free-throws following minor fouls that occur between the 6- and 9-meter lines opposite from the point of the foul. The defense must be 3 meters from the ball.

goal-area line—The 6-meter line or the circle.

goal-throw—The throw taken by the goalie from inside the goal area after the goalie deflects the ball over the goal or endline or after an attacker throws the ball over the endline.

goalkeeper restraining line—This line is 4 meters away from the rear edge of the goal line. The goalie must stand behind this line on a 7-meter throw.

long corner—The top and bottom corners of the goalpost farthest from the ball.

referee-throw—When players from both teams infringe the rules at the same time or gain simultaneous possession of a loose ball, the referee will throw the ball up between two players at center court (like a jump ball in basketball).

7-meter throw—A penalty throw awarded for serious fouls or other violations of the rules that destroy a clear scoring opportunity. 7-meter throws are taken from the 7-meter line.

short corner—The top and bottom corners of the goalpost closest to the ball.

substitution area—Substitutes must enter and leave the game from an area 4.45 meters on either side of the centerline. This designated area is located in front of the scoring table and the team benches.

throw-in—When a ball goes out of bounds across the sideline, it is put back into play from the spot where it went out of bounds. The player throwing the ball must have one foot on the sideline when taking the throw.

throw-in from the corner—A throw-in is taken from the corner of the court when a defensive player (excluding the goalie) is the last to touch the ball as it goes out of bounds over the goal line (endline).

throw-off—The throw-off is taken after the referee's whistle and is a pass to a teammate at the centerline to start the game and after each goal scored.

zone defense—A ball-orientated system in which every defender is responsible for a specific area.

SUGGESTED READINGS

Aagaar, P., and E. Skovsgaard. 1979. *Minihandball.* Roskilde, Denmark: Roas.

Atlanta Committee for the Olympic Games. 1994. *Olympic day in the schools: Sports training manual—Team handball.* Atlanta: Atlanta Committee for the Olympic Games.

Blazic, B., Z. Soric, and J. Belford, eds. 1972. *Team handball—An exciting physical fitness game for all.* Winnipeg, Manitoba: Manitoba Team Handball Federation.

British Handball Association. *Teaching team handball—Coaching manual I.* Milton Keynes, England: British Handball Association.

Canadian Team Handball Federation. 1986. *Canadian Team Handball Federation coaching manual level I.* Vanier, Ontario: Canadian Team Handball Federation.

Dwight, M.P., and K. McRae. 1980. *This is team handball.* Colorado Springs: U.S. Team Handball Federation.

Dwight, M.P., ed. 1991. *Team handball Special Olympics volunteer coach training school manual.* Washington, DC: Special Olympics International.

Garcia Cuesta, J. 1980. *Team handball technique—Coaching & methods committee.* Colorado Springs: U.S. Team Handball Federation.

Hamil, B.M., and J.D. LaPoint. 1994. *Team handball: Skills, strategies and training.* Dubuque, IA: Eddie Bowers.

Hattig, F., and P. Hattig. 1979. *Handball.* Germany: International Handball Federation and Falken Verlag.

International Handball Federation. 1983. *Handball: Sport for all.* Basel, Switzerland: International Handball Federation.

International Handball Federation. 1987. *Handball: Sport for all—technique and method.* Basel, Switzerland: International Handball Federation.

International Handball Federation. August 1, 1993. *International Handball Federation rules of the game.* Basel, Switzerland: Beckmann Druck.

Johnson, C., and G. Macdonald. 1990. *Team handball: An instructional package for coaches, teachers and recreation leaders.* New Westminster, British Columbia: Douglas College.

Marczinka, Z. 1993. *Playing handball: A comprehensive study of the game.* Budapest, Hungary: Trio Budapest.

Muhlethaler, U., and P. Raez, eds. 1977. *Handball-A.B.C.* Basel, Switzerland: International Handball Federation.

Neil, G.I. 1976. *Modern team handball—Beginner to expert.* Montreal, Quebec: McGill University.

U.S. Team Handball Federation. 1981. *Mini-manual for referees.* Short Hills, New Jersey: U.S. Team Handball Federation.